SO-ANF-103

The author pictured with her pet greater sulphur-crested cockatoo, Mr. Hopper. This bird can perform tricks such as posing like an angel (as seen here), imitating an eagle that is about to get its prey, dancing on a table or floor, and waving good-bye by flapping the right wing. The crest can be raised or lowered at will. Photo by Mr. Kruger.

Introduction
to the
Revised Edition

Mother always wanted to live in Florida or someplace else where the climate would be suitable for having her beloved birds outside all of the year, so when the Parrot Jungle offered her the job of curator of birds, she jumped at the chance. She moved her birds (almost forgetting her clothes) to Miami and spent happy, busy years supervising the diet and general management of a large family of macaws, cockatoos and various parrots.

Then she retired and settled down one and a half miles north of the Parrot Jungle, on the same road where she had passed this old farmhouse with one acre of ground. There she had her own personal parrot jungle. She had finches, love-birds, parrakeets and, of course, cockatiels. Gradually she lost interest in the smaller birds and obtained more and more of the larger birds and successfully raised some baby cocka-toos, African grey parrots and macaw babies. During this time she worked on her cockatiels and established the strain of the albino cockatiel. How she did it I do not know, as she wrote notes on everything (including the birdhouse walls), but only she could interpret the notes. She was very proud of her albino cockatiels and sold them to various breeders in Japan and other countries. Of course they are all over the world now.

Her greatest love was Mr. Hopper, a greater sulphur-crested cockatoo, who went everywhere she did. She taught him a little routine of tricks and took him around to various places to show off. He became such a ham actor that he would scream at visitors until they looked at him. She dearly loved him—he was her proudest possession.

She could pull birds through almost any illness. She removed lumps from small birds like parrakeets. All the neighborhood children and adults brought little wild birds that had fallen out of nests to her, and she fed them and released them when they were well. Once a man from Atlantic City sent his pet African grey to her by air. The parrot was so ill that he was lying on the bottom of the cage. Mother worked on him, feeding and doctoring him until he was well again. The man sent her a trophy saying, *"For Mrs. Moon— Thanks for saving my life—Joey."* She wanted to write a book on medical care for birds, but she ran out of time.

She was ill the last few years of her life, and the doctors told her she would possibly have to be confined to a wheelchair, but she still was determined to care for her birds. She spent hours working on their pens to make them more comfortable, trying new foods and handfeeding countless little cockatiels for her many customers all over the United States. She also raised baby macaws, baby African greys, and several baby cockatoos, feeding them by hand so they would be tame and then shipping them to their new owners.

Next to the cockatiels, she loved cockatoos, and she had the pleasure of owning many varieties such as Moluccans, umbrellas, citron-crested, blue-eyed, lesser and greater sulphur-crested and others.

She was totally dedicated to birds. She lived and breathed birds—her bedroom had a bed and wall to wall bird cages. The bedroom was littered with pictures, letters and bird books. Nothing mattered or interested her except birds. It was always a pleasure to me that I could do everything else (cooking, shopping, business, etc.) and she could be free in her last days to do what she loved so much. She always said she wanted to die with her boots on, and she was feeding birds two days before her death in November, 1971.

Violet Moon Wilson

Origin, color, habit

I get many letters asking what a cockatiel is and what colors they come in. Frequently I am asked if I have any white ones (confusing cockatiels with cockatoos, much larger and quite different birds, although of the same family).

I think that the cockatiel is still too close to its natural state to come in different colors, although I have had some pairs that throw very dark gray young, some very light gray, and some have very pretty yellow flecks on the breast. I had

Even in a black and white photograph the bright orange spot on the cheek is unmistakably visible. Both males and females have the spot.

one baby that had a yellow "lace" marking on each tiny feather, but he lost his coloring when he changed his baby feathers for adult male plumage. Some day, I imagine, such babies will be line-bred and new colors produced. I am cockatiel-poor, keeping so many test-mate birds for mutations. I had always mated the darkest together and the lightest together in order to have each kind to please the people. After years and years of such breeding, the cockatiels began to show more and more white about the head and neck and finally could be compared to pied parakeets. With later in-breedings of these birds, I bred birds quite like the harlequin, three-quarters or more white.

A full-grown cockie measures eleven or twelve inches from the tip of the beak to the tip of the tail. Hens are a bit shorter. Photo by John McIntosh.

This white cockie was the product of Mrs. Moon's breeding experiments. Little Hop-Along Cassidy is three-fourths white.

I'm very proud of my few whites. It's a long hard task to get them as this inbreeding must mix up the blood factors some way to make them weaker. As in humans, there are some factors that sometimes work against satisfactory reproduction of the desired results. There are heart-breaking incidents. For example, there were five beautiful babies in a nest—two whites and three normals. The three normals were as fat as butter and growing like weeds. One morning I found one white bird dead, but there was no apparent reason. In a few days, the other white was dead, while the three yellows grew on to perfection. I have one white bird now that I started to hand-feed after I saw it beg the parent birds for food. It was quite thin, and I believe it would have died if I hadn't started to hand-feed it. The bird is gaining now.

I am one who never gives up, and someday I hope I'll have what I want in these striking fellows. I suppose someone worked as hard on parakeets before the line was established. A pure white robin and an albino cardinal proved to me that painstaking breeding can accomplish certain goals. And so I feel that it is important that the readers of this book know that there are such rare and beautiful creatures on the way, even though it will be quite some time before they are plentiful.

The cockatiel is a native of Australia, but I have been able to find little information as to its origin. With the help of our librarian, I have searched our public library, but we found only one book with one sentence: "Australian cockatiels are smart birds and can be taught many tricks." Lots of help, after having raised them for years and knowing all about their clever tricks!

The nurse in the office of a doctor who has one of my cockies wrote to tell me that a young American soldier came to see the doctor and was surprised and delighted to see a cockatiel strutting around the office. He said that he had been stationed on an island off Australia and in many places the birds were as thick as the English sparrow is in the United States. In fact, he said that many of the boys in his camp had made pets of this very friendly and intelligent bird and could be seen parading through the village, each one with a pet cockie riding on his shoulder. They did not try to keep them in captivity, and often all a soldier had to do was to whistle and his "own" pet would come flying out of the forest to him.

Judging from the birds' build and actions, I should think their natural habitat was close to timber where they could bore into rotting trees for nesting, yet near enough to open plains where they could freely exercise their wings in their search for the seeds of grains or grasses. They are unusually powerful flyers, being very swift and strong. Many an unhappy owner has lost his pet by being careless about doors and unscreened windows. If a pet gets out of the house he is seldom found. He does not recognize the outside of the house and may fly ten miles before falling exhausted. So watch your pets and guard against such an accident.

A full-grown cockie is eleven to twelve inches from the tip of the beak to the tip of the tail. Hens are a bit shorter, weighing three to four ounces. They are somewhat the size of

Kurt perched on one of his trophies he received for being the best large foreign cage bird in a bird show. Kurt was one of the three little K's, Mrs. Moon's first baby cockatiels raised by hand from the shell.

the common turtle dove, but a bit more on the slender side. The adult male plumage is of rich gray body feathers. The tail is black underneath and light gray on top, and the sides of the face and throat are pure lemon yellow, with some yellow in the crest. Both sexes have a brilliant red-orange spot over each ear. They are distinguished by beautifully shaped crests which are raised or lowered according to the mood of the bird.

Both sexes have pheasant-like tails, with the two middle feathers being much longer and more slender than the rest of the tail feathers; they lie on top of the rest of the tail feathers when folded. There are twelve feathers in the tail.

Both sexes have a large patch of pure white on the lower edge of the folded wing. When they spread their wings, this white is quite striking. They have the "hooked" bill and the seemingly double-jointed feet, made for climbing, that are peculiar to birds of the parrot family (Psittacidae). Two toes turn toward the front and two toward the back. The outside back toe is longer and jointed to bend forward easily with the other two in front. When banding your cockatiels, you'll notice that the shorter inside toe bends up along the leg; if this is remembered they are easily banded when about ready to fly—at three or four weeks old—and banding should be done then, or before, so they do not notice the bands.

The female's long, dark flight feathers on her wings have yellow polka dots on them, showing only when spread, and tiny yellow bars and stripes adorn more of her body feathers, except the head and breast. Her outside tail feathers have considerable yellow and heavy black bars, but she has very little yellow about the head, eyes and throat, where His Lordship has so much. The shades and amount of yellow and spacing of bars differ in each bird.

Baby cockies all look like hens until four to six months old, when they begin to molt to adult plumage. Young males can be told before this time by their efforts to whistle, but their yellow neckline and face and their "strutting" and "hopping" are the best proof. Some little hens can fool you into believing they are males, for they try to whistle, but most hens never make the effort. If you have a nest of three or four young, their sexes can be determined more easily by comparison with each other. If you have only one, give it a mirror and you will find that a male will strut and hop to his reflection by the time he is three or four months old.

I have frequently received letters from people who have had two males or two hens for a year or more and always believed they had a pair. They write and ask me, "Why, oh why, won't they lay?" And the reason is that some dealer was not particular or did not care whether he was actually selling a pair.

Cockies are usually quite true to their mates, and it is a very hard job to break up and remate them if they are within hearing of each other. I had a very recent experience of this nature. The little hen seemed tired and worn, although her mate kept insisting on looking about for a new nest site, so I shipped him off as a loan to a friend so that the hen could rest peacefully. He was gone several months and while gone he made up with my friend's hen; they mated, but the hen did not lay. My friend was discouraged and sent both of them back to me.

The little male knew he was home as soon as he was out of the shipping box; he immediately went to his old mate, sat on the porch of their last nest box and proceeded to make violent love to her by picking around on her head and neck feathers and occasionally pulling one out. In two weeks they had eggs and were as happy as though they had never been parted. He never once paid the least attention to the hen that was sent back with him, and I do not doubt that if I had had a male here that she liked and that liked her, she, too, would have had eggs by now.

This pulling of feathers is an ugly habit of some birds. They often keep their hens looking more like scarecrows than well-dressed ladies. Some pick at the female's crest and some

Two Birdville cockatiels. Rex (left) biting the foot of Sages. This is a way of telling her he cares. Photo by B.E. Nickerson.

at her neck feathers. Two males I have seem not to approve of their wives' wearing rouge, so they pull out every red feather over their ears, yet touch no others. Perhaps that is their way of saying, "You belong to me, so no other flirtatious fellow is going to admire you."

Occasionally a hen will get even by literally snatching her mate bald-headed, but not often. Mostly they seem to feel that feather-plucking is a male privilege and put up with it. Some hens can "work" and still look pretty, but very few.

You can remate a bird if it is out of hearing of the old mate or if it is kept penned until the mate is paired up and laying, but they do show a marked preference for their own choice; I have known them to desert the mate I had picked and take another and live happily ever after. They seem to get along better with mates of their own choosing and share more of the responsibility of the family.

I had an example of this recently when a pair was brought here. The owner had had them for a year with no sign of mating. We wanted to see how they'd act here. They would sit close and seemed to think a lot of each other, but when one of my males would go into a box and whistle to his own lady, this visiting hen would fly over there and want to go in. Finally, a grown unattached male came back for resale and immediately this hen went into the box and started cleaning house and chewing up paper, and they mated. She would knock any other bird clear off the perch, and when the old mate would fly there she'd tear out as though to give battle, seeing who it was, though, she would merely bite at him gently.

The male whose female eventually mated with the male that had been returned to me for resale is still looking for a mate, but to date none will have him. Perhaps it is because he does not whistle well or has no appeal in his whistle. He tries hard; he struts and hops and shows off gayly to no avail. It looks as though he is doomed to remain a bachelor.

The male is supposed to do most of the daytime incubating and the hen the nighttime incubating—like pigeons. Some are much more helpful than others, and some seem to

Cockies will not hesitate to get wet in a dish or pan of water. They prefer best of all, however, to be sprinkled lightly with water as if they are under a shower or rain.

love the companionship of their mates so much that both set a great deal. Especially is this so when the babies first arrive. The parents act as if they are so proud they can hardly trust the precious things to the other one's care, and one will be found on the babies and the other on the rest of the eggs.

After the babies are quite large or do not need covering at night, the hen sits at the door of the box, on guard, as long as they stay in it. At the least unusual noise in the dark, she is ready to hiss, scold and flap, generally hanging head down with tail spread like a fan over the door and wings and mouth ready for action on the intruder. When I take the babies away to hand-feed, often my pet hens insist on coming into the living room to sit on top of the box where I have put them, so faithful are they to their young.

The male pays no attention to them at this age, except to help feed in the daytime. All the males go to roost at night near one another, and each has his favorite place on the perch. They carry in nesting material but like something to chew up in the box, so I give cardboard or paper or some such material to imitate the hollow-tree homes in their native land as well as I can. This might all sound very foolish to some, but I do know that if your cockies are not healthy, contented, and happy—you won't get babies.

BATHING. . .

Cockies are not proficient bathers like canaries or Java rice birds. They look very awkward as they dig their heads in the pan and shake the water off or sit in it and get their breasts a little wet. They dearly love a warm, gentle April shower and want to bathe in it. It is a pretty sight to see four or five lying on the windowsill or on a cage in front of it, holding up first one wing and then the other, trying to capture every possible drop. Pet cockies can be trained to be unafraid of a spray from the faucet and will come to the sink and beg for a bath. They will roll on my hand and lift every feather so that the water can reach the skin as I sprinkle it on them. They do this only when they are in the mood, however, and not always at the owner's convenience, often deciding to have a bath when you are in the midst of cooking a meal. The quickest way out of this is to give them a little quick wetting and send them to the bird room to dry and preen, and you can still be assured they will have had a better bath than they would have had if they had taken it in a pan.

AGE. . .

I do not personally know of any cockies much over ten years of age, although I have no reason to doubt that they live much longer; they belong to a "long-lived" bird family. The birds I have known that were ten years old are still hale and hearty although retired from the breeding list. Daddy Jake died at a *known* age of fourteen—he may have been older—not sick, smooth and beautiful as ever, just plain old age.

When I came to Florida in 1952, I presented Peekaboo and his mate, Kay, to the Parrot Jungle. They were beautiful, but I had supposed them too old to breed. Two and a half years later, they presented the Jungle with five of the most beautiful babies anyone has ever seen, and at the time of the mating Peekaboo was fifteen and Kay was thirteen. Through them Birdville's line will carry on at Parrot Jungle for years to come. Kay died at fifteen and Peekaboo died at eighteen.

PEACEFUL BIRDS. . .

Cockatiels are very peaceful birds, often eating out of the same dish with the tiniest of finches or parrakeets. In fact, a parrakeet can pester the life out of a cockie if it takes a notion. I once had a pair of cockies raising six or seven little 'keets. When weaning them, I put them in the same cage with a half dozen more from a pair of 'keets. The male cockie and the female 'keet really fought over those babies, each laying claim to the whole bunch and each trying to feed them through the wires. They would fly to the ceiling, each trying to get above the other for a final clinch. When they would get a hold on each other, they would fall to the floor with a bang and hold on like bulldogs until I would come and separate them. I thought I would have to make other arrangements to keep peace in the family, but while I was figuring out what and how, and they were having one battle after another, with me scolding and separating, I noticed that they were finally growing a bit tired of their squabble; the parrakeet would run behind the cage to feed the babies, while the cockie would sit on the wide ledge in front. So I just kept my eye on them; if they got too close, the cockie would scream and then I'd scold him and each would run to his own side. So they finally learned to work with one on each side of the cage, keeping a watchful eye on each other along with some pretty cross looks. Of course, all this was dealing with two pets; perhaps I would never have had such an experience with wild ones.

If two males happen to want to use the same nest box, they can also put up a battle with each other and sometimes ruin a nest of eggs (although I have never lost any babies this way). Both babies and adults, when not too angry, will fight by biting each other's feet and legs. They realize they can't make much impression just standing up and batting beaks together. When they really mean business, they fly up at each other and believe me, the feathers can fly. It is quite a job to keep peace among ten or twelve pairs loose in a room seven by thirteen feet.

When a baby begins to come out of the nest box (they usually do this with an aimless bang against the window or the floor), the parent birds are more than likely to hit the floor ahead of it and guard it there until I rescue it and return it to the nest.

These birds do not like any changes in their homes. They know and prefer their own cages. I ask anyone bringing me birds to take care of while they are away on vacation, or if I am to keep a sick bird for observation (especially then), to bring the bird's own cage along. The birds remain much happier and satisfied in their familiar quarters.

I recently bought back a pair I had sold as babies, because their owner could no longer keep them. They had lived in one big cage for so long that they were very unhappy for weeks. They would pace back and forth and fuss and cry with homesickness, especially when bedtime came.

Cockies are very intelligent birds, and each one has its own individual personality and disposition. Some cockatiels are very friendly with almost anyone; some are distinctly one-man birds; some have sweet dispositions, and nothing could make them bite their owners; and others, while good and very affectionate most of the time, will not hesitate to "bite the hand that feeds them" if things just don't suit them.

All in all, of my whole aviary, containing all kinds and colors, shapes and sizes of birds, I prefer the handsome cockatiel. I can cheerfully recommend a tame, hand-raised cockatiel as the perfect house pet—a bird that should be in every home where there is a bird lover. By bird lover I mean one who really loves a bird for itself and not just to ornament the house, to sit in a pretty cage and accentuate the decorations of a room or to show off to friends, but one who wants a bird to love and cherish for its beauty and its cunning ways, and above all for its deep affection for its owner.

Jake & Judy —
my first cockatiels

I had seen this pair of birds a number of times and admired them very much. I didn't dream that I would ever own them or that the owner would think of parting with them. I well knew that if they were mine I would never give them up.

However, the owner preferred canaries and with the winter coming on, she decided to sell the cockatiels. And when she made me the offer, I lost no time in saying yes before she could change her mind. I proudly carried my lovely birds home and when my husband looked them over, he wondered what I had seen in them—such somber-coated fellows, so wild and biting and hissing. But like the husbands of many bird lovers, I guess he thought "anything to make her happy" and offered no objections.

I was so happy and thrilled over my new pets—and I might add that I have never gotten over being thrilled with each and every one I've owned since, and I even enjoy caring for an extra cage or two for others. In sight of the chair where I am now writing there are eighteen of my own and four boarders, with perhaps another dozen adults and several nests of babies and eggs in the bird room. I have counted as many as thirty-five from this same chair.

Jake was a beautiful bird. His head was nearly orange instead of lemon. He was eleven and one-half inches long. His crest was particularly beautiful, long and curved, and he raised or lowered it continually to express his emotions. Judy was the largest and longest hen I have ever seen, but so terribly wild. I was never able to tame her even a little. She was like, I imagine, a wild captive taken from her jungle home. She was a very dark, drab color with scarcely a tinge of yellow anywhere except in her tail. Together they weighed one-half pound, Judy being the heavier.

I planned and fixed things for them and fed and cared for them as the original owner had instructed me, just feeling my way in the dark as it were. They had a large cage and a nest box (in which she had had fertile eggs often but never a live baby). I could scarcely eat or sleep I was so interested in watching them.

The cage seemed small, and when I thought of the long miles of flight they would have had in their native haunts, I would let them out for a half hour or so each day. They would hang head down with those pretty graceful wings and tails spread as though trying to show me how beautiful they really were. They would hold on to the cage, or more often on top of the curtains, with their strong feet and flap their wings vigorously for exercise (a trait of all cockatiels).

So as the days went by I built up great hopes that they would do more than just lay eggs for me. I expected them to like their new home and partial freedom enough to set and hatch their eggs in proper fashion. I had raised many canaries in my life, but I realized no matter how beautifully they

A full length picture of Jake, one of Birdville's original pair of cockatiels.

sing or how tame they may become, a canary could never fill the place that a cockatiel does. And these were only a pair of wild birds that could not be handled without getting your fingers torn, and I did not yet know of the joy of owning a tame one that could be picked up at will and loved and petted, or that would love me enough to come flying in from the bird room and perch on my shoulders and walk about on my lap-board as I write—like several inquisitive fellows are doing at this moment.

Well, I hovered around those birds doing everything for their comfort and well-being that I could think of, although I know now it was mostly all wrong. And even though my friend had had them for several years and no babies were hatched, I just couldn't believe but that I would have some when my Judy laid seven eggs. Of course, I then knew nothing about a grit and sod and mineral tray, as I later found out about. I could find nothing to read on the breeding of cockatiels, except that somewhere in my searchings I did read something that made me realize their nest box was far too small.

I worked most of a day making a new nest box with a saucer-like place in the bottom (and only an old wood chisel to work with). I put the dished-out place in the center as the article said, and that was *not* where Judy wanted her eggs. She would try to roll them into the corner farthest from the door—she would get two or three there and sit on them while the rest of her eggs lay in the hollowed out place. I worked another half day to fix the hollow where she wanted it. Well, they greatly enjoyed a box large enough for both to get into at once, but it did not help matters a great deal. This was not the real cause of the trouble.

Judy would set about a week, then quit for two or three days, then perhaps she would set again after the eggs were ruined. I tried penning her in the box at night. I tried covering the cage, as I thought perhaps the lights being turned on and off disturbed her. Nothing I could do would keep her setting. Nest after nest of eggs was ruined. Her droppings would get very thin and foul-smelling, then she would desert her eggs.

Once a kind friend made me a little incubator out of a light bulb and cracker can. I tried to finish the eggs in it but the moisture and heat control were not perfect enough—the young picked the shell but died there. After many such disappointments, the light finally dawned and I knew that the reason Judy was not setting was that she was sick and that it was the laying and setting that made her sick.

I noticed she would eat all the dry droppings off the paper if I did not get them out in time, so I knew she needed something I had not provided in her diet. While trying to figure out what it could be, I remembered that while I was living in Oklahoma, my pigeons would come around a little tree we were trying to nurse along through drought and wind by pouring our dish water at its roots. The whole flock of pigeons would come there and eat heartily of that damp earth. I assumed they were eating the dirt because of the salt and grease in it, so I decided to try to get my cockies back nearer to nature.

I got a tray of grit with some bonemeal, limestone, charcoal and a piece of sod, one corner of which I soaked in salt water. I put the tray on a table and opened the door of the cage. I was rewarded because both Jake and Judy took to the addition to their diet immediately, and I soon noticed that each clutch of eggs was cared for a little longer.

Then Judy found a nail hole in the plaster and chewed a big place all around it—showing me that she would like and needed more than egg-shells and cuttlebone to make big eggs. So I supplied her with oyster-shell, pieces of old plaster, and plaster-board; I also found that she liked a piece of old yellow or "soft" brick pounded up. I have since worked out a fine grit formula and I also give my breeders a salt spool made for rabbits. This is rather hard, so I soak it in water at times, or at least a corner of it. I later learned that ordinary iodized table salt and a bit of calcium in a little dish works very well. Use a calcium with vitamin D in it.

Poor Judy was laying right along, even with the wrong diet to make eggs. The drain on her system was too much, so although I was doing the best I knew or could find out from others, the poor little lady died from being egg-bound while trying to lay her fiftieth egg since I had brought her home—and leaving me with the last clutch.

Poor little Judy, a martyr to my ignorance. My only consolation was that I tried, and through the process of trial and error I may now pass on to others the things I have since learned in hope that it will help them save their Judys.

The following grit formula has helped very much to prevent eggbinding by supplying the needs of laying hens. Don't waste it by spreading it on the floor. If you want sand on the floor, use common sand or ordinary commercial grit, but keep a real mineral grit before them at all times. Your pet shop will sell nationally distributed grit. *Sand is not enough.* The formula below makes over five pounds and will last a year for one pair.

> 1 lb. fine oyster shell
> 1 lb. powdered oyster shell
> 1/8 lb. medium fine charcoal
> 1½ lb. clean sand or pigeon grit
> 5 oz. ground bonemeal
> 4 oz. ground limestone
> 4 oz. iodized salt
> ¼ of an old soft brick pounded fine

Your pet shop can furnish most of these ingredients; better yet, pet shops sell packaged products specifically designed to provide a good grit mix. Another help for egg-binding is two or three tablespoons of lime water to each pint of water. A tube makes one gallon and is sold in drug stores, or you can buy it already made up.

At sea

If other cockatiel breeders have ever worried and worked and tried harder than I did to know what to do for their birds and were still as much "at sea" as I was, I certainly have great respect for their patience and perseverance and would like to have a chance to meet and talk it over.

After the incubator failure, the next deserted eggs were carried to a pigeon man who set them, but as I could not talk to him personally at the time, he did not understand clearly what kind of birds they were and he expected the pigeons to feed them without his notifying me.

Then he offered to lend me a pair of pure white doves that had been living in a coop out-of-doors. When I brought them home and fixed them up in the warm bird room (it was very cold outside), I guess they thought spring had come suddenly, and they went to work at once.

You can't imagine how excited I was! When the first egg was laid in the poorly constructed nest of the doves, Prince and Pearly, it was replaced by one of Judy's. This was on January second. On January fourth another exchange. On the sixth and seventh I added two more, fearing if I put all in at once Pearly might not like it. Four was all she could cover, as only two eggs are usually in a dove's clutch.

It was bitterly cold, and I wondered if they could cover four eggs safely, but you have never seen anything more faithful than this pair of doves. They seemed to know it was very cold and took no risks. Pearly would set all night until about eight in the morning, which gave Prince time to stuff himself with food and water. Then he would carefully sneak up to the nest and stand on the edge for a while, as if to ask for the privilege of his turn on those precious eggs. They would then trade places so carefully I could scarcely get a glimpse of the eggs. Pearly would stretch her legs and wings and eat and drink and lie in the sun on the window sill. Between four and five in the afternoon, they would exchange places again for the night. With what anxious care I watched every move as my final hope of baby cockatiels was now entrusted to their care!

On January eighth I could not wait any longer. I just had to get my fingers on those eggs. Sure enough—the first two showed fertility. Now more than ever did I hope those doves would prove faithful.

Perhaps you would like to know how to test eggs. I have tested incubators full so many times (chickens, ducks, and turkeys) that I can tell at a glance by just holding up the egg in the sunlight or before an electric light bulb. Some use the method of taking a black cardboard and cutting a hole in it a bit smaller than the egg. This helps you to see better by shielding the eyes. A more elaborate tester is a little box with

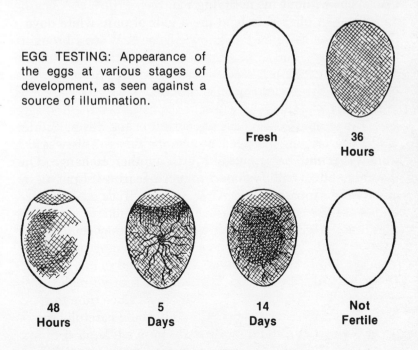

EGG TESTING: Appearance of the eggs at various stages of development, as seen against a source of illumination.

Fresh

36 Hours

48 Hours

5 Days

14 Days

Not Fertile

a light bulb inside and holes smaller than the eggs on top—lay the eggs on the holes and look through them. There will be a small dark speck and red veins running in all directions, somewhat like a little spider at first.

Each day the chick grows larger until the egg is well filled and dark except for an air space at the large end. If for any reason the chick dies in the shell, part will be clear and there will be a dark lump. If after three to six days the egg still looks perfectly clear, it is infertile and no good. It will not rot, however, but will remain like a fresh egg even though set on for the full time of incubation.

On January twelfth I tested again. The last two eggs were well started; the first two were coming right along and the doves were surely doing their part. Such thoughts ran through my mind as I went about my neglected housework. Will they continue now?

January sixteenth. Still on the job! January eighteenth. A raging sub-zero blizzard, so cold I didn't see how anything could hatch, but I was afraid to disturb Prince and Pearly long enough for a peek.

In those days I had no knowledge of how long it took to hatch the eggs, and so I had to wait and watch. I gave them fresh water often so it would not get too cold, as it was impossible in this awful storm to heat the house, let alone the bird room.

It was now sixteen days since the first egg was put under and I was on pins and needles. My one thought was—will I finally get my baby cockies? One guess was as good as another, but I had prepared myself not to be surprised at another disappointment. After all the trials and blasted hopes of the past months, instead of feeling "I *will* get babies this time," I felt more like "It would be too good to be true."

Yes! I did get babies

On January twenty-eighth I took one last look before going to bed. I heard a tiny "peep peep," so even though it was still cold, I risked looking at the eggs and sure enough, one peeped. I could hardly wait for morning to come so I could see him.

How disappointed I was when I found he was still in the shell—and he stayed there all day! I had to go to bed another night without a glimpse of him. You can imagine how I hurried to the bird room on the morning of January thirtieth— and there I found him, my first look at the cutest, sweetest (yet homely) little fellow I ever owned.

He was all covered with yellow fuzz (not naked like a parrakeet baby) except for his head and neck, which were nearly bare and somewhat resembled a little turtle's head and neck. Not pretty really, but beautiful to me. Prince and Pearly had done a very good job getting them out in only eighteen days when I have had cockies take one-half to one day longer.

And now I was in a predicament! The first "tiny" I had ever seen and I knew absolutely nothing about how or what to feed it and no way to find out. Well, mine has always been an inventive and experimental nature, so I went at it. I was afraid if I took the baby away it might cause the doves to leave the nest; I also thought they could keep the best temperature. They were quite used to my bothering them by now, and I decided to feed the baby and let them brood as, of course, they could not feed infant cockatiels.

A mother dove opens her mouth and the baby (often two babies at once, one on each side) sticks its bill in her mouth; she pumps up their food from her craw and they draw it in at the same time. A baby cockie knows nothing of this system of feeding, nor would its hooked bill have worked if it had. Parent cockies hook their bills in that of the baby and shake him, gently when little, but quite hard when bigger. Perhaps it is the baby that does the shaking (they do it when hand-fed), and, of course, the baby helps by drawing the food down.

Well, I had hardly gotten started on this little fellow when I had my next disappointment. Pearly wanted very much to feed it, and she would coax it out and try; finally it tumbled over the edge of the nest into the corner of the box and was chilled in a few minutes. I warmed it up, but it died even before the next one came out of the egg. I feared to try that on the next baby, so I fixed up a little cracker can incubator into a brooder by tearing up an old brass canary cage and using the foot on the bottom of it for a deflector, putting a bulb and thermometer and filling it partly full of very fine shavings (and sometimes wheat bran). Then I cooked and strained the food I had decided to try, and when the next little bird came, I started in on my job. And the most exciting

The cockatiel lowers and raises its crest depending on the mood it is in. Photo by Bill Ziske.

time of my life was, I think, when I really saw some food go down that baby's craw.

Three weeks later a reporter came out and took a photo of Daddy Jake and the three babies and put an article in our local newspaper about my experiences in raising the first Australian cockatiels in my city.

I carefully marked each baby on its wing or head with Mercurochrome, my old standby for marking eggs and babies. As they hatch nearly two days apart, they always stay that much ahead of each other in size. I had to find names that would do for either sex, since it could not be told, so I decided on Koxy, Kewpie, and Kurt.

Unless you love the handling of birds as much as I do you will never know the pleasure and enjoyment I had out of those first babies. I was, by this time, convinced that I would now have live tame birds to hold and love, and to really love me, and not just tolerate me while I cuddled them. To say they have fulfilled every longing is to put it mildly.

Well, the three little yellow fluff balls were a great responsibility at first. Their food had to be prepared carefully and warmed each time in clean pans. Thirty years ago I had raised my two baby girls on the bottle and their bottles were not better sterilized—nor was their diet more closely watched. I had to feed every hour! It seemed as if I had time for nothing else between feedings, but I felt that when at long last I had three baby cockatiels, I simply had to make a success of raising them.

I ground some nestling food very fine and chewed it up until warm and well mixed with saliva, then I took a bit of this warm gruel and fed from my fingers and variously devised feeders. I wiped their little faces off, thankful they were at least bare of down or feathers on neck and face. Then I put them to bed in the little brooder.

When they were nearly two weeks old, I thought I could stretch the feeding time, but it was too soon and the two smallest, Kurt and Kewpie, had sour crops within thirty-six hours from being so hungry and taking too much food at a time. I learned that *little* and *often* is the best rule. I found the food was not passing on as it should, so two droppers full

A cock usually appears in better physical condition than a hen. Males pull off certain feathers from the females causing their plumage to appear very scraggly and worn. Photo by Harry Lacey.

of warm water were put down each tiny crop, and the babies were held upside down over the sink and the soured food washed out. I washed their crops again with warm water and put one full dropper down to stay, containing a tiny bit of Eno salts or three drops of cremo carbonates.

Next morning they were ready for breakfast, but you can be sure it was back to hourly feedings. The only other time I had any worry was when they were quite a good size and I felt that they needed seed, as I knew the parents give it very early. So I tried grinding millet and blowing the hulls off the best I could and adding this to their gruel. I had to discontinue this practice, however, as once again they went off appetite. We now have "peeled" millet which is a great help; it can be ground and fed even when the birds are very tiny, or even fed whole.

Outside of these two times, both my fault, I have never seen baby cockatiels grow better, whether fed by hand or parents, and I felt quite proud of my three little K's, especially since after Judy's death there was no hope of any more eggs. After three weeks I stretched out the feedings to four or five times a day; by this time they were shelling seed and picking at greens and egg food for themselves.

I had been keeping them in a shallow box where they could see me and look around, but at about four weeks I gave them their first lesson in clinging to my shoulders. At first they were afraid of falling and hugged tightly against my neck—and how those "needles" in their toes did stick and scratch. But they soon learned what it was all about and were as much at home on me as in the box. They would ride by the hour, sleeping or picking and playing with each other or the trinkets I pinned on my dress for that purpose.

They learned a cute trick to keep from being disturbed when they were sleepy. They ran down on my back when I stooped over, and up again when I straightened up. They just went down and sat one on each hip, or if my apron had a big bow, sometimes one or two perched on it. I kept them on me so much I hardly knew they were there. I made a little cape of an old seersucker dress to keep my shoulders clean, but I assure you I always get the "dirty end of the deal" when I am taming cockies. After they grow up and are off so much soft food they are exceptionally clean birds and seldom have an accident while riding on your shoulder.

By now my three K's were through with the little brooder, and they had a warm, tight box to sleep in. When I went out they were tucked in it with a dish of food beside them and went along with me—even taking a long automobile ride when about four weeks old.

In the evenings they played about me on an old armchair like kittens, and many hours were made happier and more cheerful by their little lives. Once a pet parrakeet lived with them for a while. He went in and out of their cage at will through the bars. As 'keets usually are, he was a mischievous little pest. He would sing and bob his head at them and chase them down the chair to the very edge of the arm. When the cockie could go no farther, it would turn on the 'keet and chase him all the way up the chair again. As each cockie has a different disposition, the 'keet soon learned which one he could torment the most, and it was poor little Koxy who received his unwanted attentions. The others paid so little attention to him they were not molested so long as Koxy was about.

My next trouble was to determine their sex. I, of course, had no knowledge or literature to help me, so I just had to watch and wait. One day the eldest made a noise which I thought must be their song, so I decided I had at least one male—but it proved to be the only little lady, my Koxy. She and Kurt were such fast friends, always close together, loving each other and scratching heads.

From the first Kewpie was everybody's friend and would far rather be with us than with the other birds, going to anyone who held out a hand for him. Kurt was not quite so friendly, but he had a very good-natured, kind disposition. While he would rather be playing about in his own way, he never objected to our changing his plans. Koxy was an independent, sassy old girl, very partial to me, and while she enjoyed riding about on my shoulders by the hour, she preferred less loving and cuddling than the other two.

THE WORLD'S LARGEST SELECTION OF PET, ANIMAL, AND MUSIC BOOKS.

T.F.H. Publications publishes more than 900 books covering many hobby aspects (dogs, cats, birds, fish, small animals, music, etc.). Whether you are a beginner or an advanced hobbyist you will find exactly what you're looking for among our complete listing of books. For a free catalog fill out the form on the other side of this page and mail it today.

. . CATS . . .

. . . BIRDS . .

. . . ANIMALS . . .

. . . DOGS . . .

. . FISH . . .

. . . MUSIC . . .

For more than 30 years, *Tropical Fish Hobbyist* has been the source of accurate, up-to-the-minute, and fascinating information on every facet of the aquarium hobby.

Join the more than 50,000 devoted readers worldwide who wouldn't miss a single issue.

RETURN TO: *Prices subject to change without notice*

Tropical Fish Hobbyist, P.O. Box 427, Neptune, NJ 07753-0427

YES! Please enter my subscription to *Tropical Fish Hobbyist*. Payment for the length I've selected is enclosed. U.S. funds only.

CHECK ONE:
☐ 1 year-$15.00   ☐ 2 years-$26.00   ☐ 3 years-$40.00   ☐ 5 years-$64.00
12 BIG ISSUES   24 ISSUES   36 ISSUES   60 ISSUES
☐ SAMPLE ISSUE-$2.00 Please allow 4-6 weeks for your subscription to start.

☐ GIFT SUBSCRIPTION. Please send a card announcing this gift. I would like the card to read_____

SEND TO:
Name_____

Street_____ Apt. No._____

City_____ State _____ Zip _____
Canada and Foreign add $6.00 per year.

Charge my: ☐ VISA   ☐ MASTER CHARGE   ☐ PAYMENT ENCLOSED

_____
Card Number   Expiration Date

_____
Cardholder's Name (if different from "Ship to:")

_____
Cardholder's Address (if different from "Ship to:")

_____
                                          Cardholder's Signature

☐ **Please send me your free catalog.**

My new Judy
starts housekeeping

After the loss of my first Judy, poor Jake nearly went wild with grief. He would chew himself out of any cage made of wood, and when I finally put him in a chew-proof cage with a few parrakeets, hoping that they would be company for him, he paced back and forth, biting the wires and screaming at any 'keet that got in his way until I was almost as frantic as he.

I showed him the babies, but no, he was afraid of them, and who could blame him—the homely little fellows! But when their needle-like quills fluffed out into real feathers, he thought they looked more like cockatiels than any other bird around and finally begged to be allowed to sleep in their cage.

In the evening we would let them walk about the floor in their queer little awkward paddling way, and he would go through all kinds of antics, hopping, strutting and whistling to them. It was then, for the first time, that my husband became charmed by my cockatiels, and of course all bird-loving women know what a boost to their morale it is when friend husband learns to like what is usually considered one of the reasons why men leave home. Unless, as it sometimes is, *he* is the bird lover—then I feel sorry for the housekeeper; birds and neat housekeeping don't go together, and they make a lot of extra work.

But I say that you should be patient and forebearing if you are married to a "bird lover"—there are lots worse things, and if you can enjoy them together, you will find them a real bond for companionship. Medical science has proved that a hobby of any kind is one of the best nerve stabilizers of all.

Well, I hunted everywhere for a mate for Jake, and at last I found, not a hen, but a pair. To get the hen I had to take both. He was the sorriest looking specimen I had ever seen—old and bald and lame, with a bill so long he could not eat, and it was no wonder that the pretty little hen paid no more attention to him after she saw my beautiful Jake. I was really glad when the poor old fellow died a few weeks later, as he still tried to call her to him with what little voice he had left.

It seemed like a case of love at first sight with both Jake and his new Judy, and in a very short time they had four eggs. Jake was like an old man with a sweet young wife whom he could not baby enough. He could put a lot of human husbands to shame, he was so considerate and tender with her.

He is just as faithful and as careful of her today as that first day I brought her home to him. In the morning, he is the first of all the males to be back in the box on duty for the day, and in the evening he is the last to come out. And if, as so often happens, I turn on the light in the bird room, he immediately goes in and wants her to come out to rest.

When babies hatch he is so careful of them that he often stays in the nest box a night or two at first, as though he can't trust her to do it right. With her first nest of eggs, she, too, was egg-bound and almost died laying her fourth egg. I had to give her a half hour of steaming; I put her in a box and hung it over the stove to keep her warm during the night.

When I steam an egg-bound hen, I hold my hands under her with fingers spread so the steam penetrates her feathers, yet with no danger of burning her, as I can tell from experience exactly how close to hold her. Another method is to put hot water in a deep pan and tie a cloth over the top and set her on it; you can also use a hot water bottle covered with cloth—anything to relax the hen. Drugs can also be used as a last resort, but I will discuss these in a later chapter.

I thought surely I would lose Judy's first eggs, but I was lucky. Daddy Jake stayed right on the job. He sat on those precious eggs nearly forty-eight hours alone, coming out only two or three times to grab a few seeds and a drink of water. When I took the box down from the stove the next morning and Judy hissed at me, I never had heard a more welcome sound, for I was much afraid I would find her stiff and cold. I cooled her off gradually, and she finally went in the box and laid the fourth egg.

Judy has never been a very prolific hen. She has never laid over four or five eggs. But they are such a dear pair of birds, and feed and care for the little ones they do have so wonderfully, I'd sooner have my Jake and Judy if they would bring me only one from a nest, than to have "just cockatiels" if they brought eight or nine. I love my birds for themselves alone and money could not buy this particular pair. Yet some folks have said to me, "Let me have Jake and Judy. You know how to train them and can train yourself another pair." They don't seem to understand that to me there are no more Jakes and Judys and this is their home for life.

They are getting old, I imagine, although I do not know the age of either, but they went through their last molt, are in fine condition, and at the present time are on four eggs. And sometimes when Jake gets to dancing about, mocking a little parrakeet in both actions and song to perfection, he seems gay and young again. He seems to disapprove of his Judy wearing "rouge." He sits and loves her and then picks a red feather off her face, so she seldom has any. But this is his only unkind act and Judy and I forgive him.

But woe betide any bird who dares to land on his front porch. Then none are too big and none too small for him to go after. (If ever a bird can "frown" it is a cockatiel.) Although the bird room can be full of loose canaries or 'keets or tiny finches, he never bothers one of them except at his own door.

Yes, my new Judy has been a perfect success and in every way satisfactory to both Jake and myself. Her first nest was only one baby—a sweet little hen I named "Buggles," and I'll tell you more about her later. In her second nest, also one baby, was "Scrappy," who lived up to his name toward most people.

After I had quite a few young ones and began to dispose

of them, it was soon noised around that my cockies were tame, so people would want to buy them before they were old enough to go. Jake and Judy couldn't bring them fast enough. At one time, some people ordered a pair just when Jake and Judy were about ready to lay and it was worse than counting your chickens before they hatched. I told Judy she must not let me down—and she didn't. She brought just two, *and a pair!*

People were so interested in the idea of tame birds that I was full of curiosity as to how much difference there was between a tame baby bird and a wild one. I had at that time a large white cockatoo who was so jealous of my pets it was not safe to keep them in the same room lest she break their legs if they got on her cage. I decided to ship the cockatoo to California and see what I could get in trade.

I received eight baby cockies, supposed to be eight males, but again proving my own experience in two things— you can't guess the sex at that age and they are generally evenly divided as to sex. I got four hens and four males. They were just babies, barely old enough to make the trip, and could they bite! They were very scared, poor little fellows.

Their lessons began that very night. Each had its wings clipped and was left to fly just enough for a bit of exercise after the long trip in the box; they also learned that they could not fly well with clipped wings. Then I fed them and put them to bed to rest.

The next day, four at a time were taken out with my bare hands (gloves often scare a bird) and set on my shoulders and made to ride there for an hour. This was done each day, several times a day, and after a few days they were not so quick to bite when I put them back in the cage, but every time I reached in to take them out, I'd get torn and bleeding fingers. This went on for several weeks. But after a couple of months they seldom bit me, at least not hard enough to bleed, but they never did like me as well as my tame ones do.

While I kept one pair of these birds and I think a great deal of these two, I found out to my entire satisfaction why people love my tame birds and why a hand-tamed bird will be more likely to make itself at home and to breed for you.

Tame cockies have no fear of individuals they grew up with. They become accustomed to the voice and movements of their trainer and his family.

Breeding, care and housing

Probably the most ideal setting to breed cockatiels, as well as most other foreign birds, would be the large outdoor aviary. That, however, would be possible only in warm climates, for while they can be hardened to stand quite a lot of cold, they are still tropical birds. I personally haven't the heart to make mine stand a temperature I would not be comfortable in myself. Some breeders do, however, and I have been asked why their cockatiels will not breed in February and March as canaries do, since they had been flying loose all winter on a big screened porch. Imagine having such expectations in Ohio's *zero* weather.

Well, we can't all have a California or Florida climate, so we must make the best of what we have. Some breeders put their birds outside in the summer and take them inside in the winter. I, too, used to think it would be nice to have an outdoor bird house, but not anymore. Since hearing all the worries and troubles so many breeders have experienced with outside aviaries because of rats, mice, dogs, cats, cold, dampness, illness, etc., and, when trying to heat them, of stoves exploding, or fires going out, or losing sleep wondering if it has gone out—I prefer mine inside with me.

They are such nervous, excitable birds that an airplane, a boy flying a kite, or a wild bird flying by outside the window will start my whole flock on a mad stampede. It is easy to see why putting them outside constantly upsets them. It would take most of the summer to get them settled outside, and when you took them in for the winter you would find broken wings, twisted legs, and toes off, rendered unfit for sale or breeding.

A cockie hates a change in his home more than any

Although of adequate size, this nest box can be greatly improved by the addition of a nest frame in one of the corners. Enough nesting materials, such as sawdust, wood shavings, straw, hay, shredded paper, etc., should be included in the nest box.

other bird I know. If I take one out of a cage and put him in another cage in the same room, he is unhappy. That's why I feel more than sorry to ship them off to their new homes and surroundings, knowing that they will sulk and droop for two or three weeks until they get used to their new home.

As cockies seem to like to start breeding in the fall, I let them, and then for the rest period during the hot months I put them out on a big screened porch. I live in an upstairs apartment where nothing can bother them but the owls. Two of the windows in my bedroom open onto this porch and at the first sign of flight, I switch on the light so they can see to find their perches and get settled again without bang-ing around and being hurt. Then, too, I can hear and see their quarrels and help settle them.

This porch is twenty feet long, and when I first put the birds out there I did lose some parrakeets who flew so hard they broke their necks. To avoid this happening to my cockies, I divided the porch into three sections. If the flying space is not too long they don't get such a fast start and hit so hard.

When they are not on the porch they are in the bird room. At first, each pair had a cage, and the doors were open all the time for the ones that did not quarrel—the quarrelsome ones being let out only for occasional exercise. But since I now have so many birds, most of them have never known what it means to be caged, and the cages are reserved for some real bad boy who insists on having the other fellow's house.

Usually, if penned until the other pair gets eggs, they'll defend their house. However, until the cockies get the full clutch of eggs laid and start setting in earnest, I keep a close watch on them. From their noises and scoldings I know just about what is going on in the bird room and will often hurry to their rescue, even from my meals, when no one else would guess that anything was wrong.

If you can't have a regular bird room and the full freedom of it, the next best thing is the largest cage possible, letting the birds have as many flights out of the cage as you can each day. If you are too particular about your home to permit this, better not try breeding, for they are messy when setting, and if allowed out a lot they may chew up lamp shades, etc.

Occasionally a pair will breed in a cage and never be allowed out, but these are exceptions rather than the rule. Usually, if a pair is shut up in a small cage, the hen will no doubt try to lay, and not having enough room or right surroundings she is likely to become egg-bound and die. Then the male will be so grieved he will nearly drive you frantic screaming and calling for her. Some pairs I have seen breed without flights have become completely useless. After doing very well the first year and fairly well the second, they never again have babies. Some of them didn't even try to lay again.

So it all depends on whether your love for birds and the joy you get out of breeding them and watching them raise their cute babies means enough to you to sacrifice your house, or at least one room of your house. And if not, it would be best to have a male bird only. Of course, a hen makes just as sweet a pet, but the male can talk and whistle. And when you are not loving and playing with him or watching his antics, he can be kept in a smaller cage with less harm than the laying breeding hen.

MAKING YOUR CAGE. . .

A canary cage is not large enough for a single cockatiel. He will be miserable in it and break his beautiful tail; the door is not large enough for him to get in and out comfortably. There are cages designed especially for cockies now on the market. They have horizontal wires on front and back, as any cage for hook-bills should be constructed. Why people expect these poor birds to live in a canary cage is more than I can understand. A canary flits from perch to perch, and it makes no difference how the wires are, but a hook-billed bird uses them to climb on. The wires should go across like the rungs of a ladder so he can walk up as if on one. I have seen a cockie grip with his beak and claws as best he could and slip and slide till worn out. It was in this way, in a large parrot cage with vertical wires that two little cockies were hanged. They got their heads through and couldn't grip the wires tight enough to climb up and get their heads out again. The cage which I designed is the smallest any cockie should be made to live in. It has a drop door for a landing porch; it is finished in chrome with a stand to match.

If you cannot buy a cage large enough and you are at all handy with tin snips and pliers, you can make a very serviceable and attractive cage from welded wire (one by two-inch mesh); the larger mesh shows the bird up better, and if painted black shows him still better. Be sure the paint is well dried before putting the bird in the cage. To brighten up the cage it can be trimmed in colors with decals on cups and mirror. Always give your cockie a mirror. He will love it, and in a way it makes up for the fact that he has no other bird to play with. One-by-two wire makes a nice ladder for their climbing.

I plan and make my own cages. I have the studding all measured and the nails in, and then I need only a very little help to hang them in place, in every available space from floor to ceiling of the bird room. I also make my own shipping crates, whether of cardboard cartons, wood, or a combination of both. All kinds of drinkers and feeders, lots of them from tin cans, are easily made and very handy as they hook in the wires of the cage and don't interfere with cleaning the floor. When you have a great many birds, it saves time not to have a lot of dishes to move when in a hurry to grab papers out of a row of cages. Some babies even get the habit of sleeping in their tin cans. I shipped one little fellow who insisted on sleeping in his seed dish at night, and I had to send directions so the new owner could make him a bed out of a tomato can. He sleeps in it every night on a bed of straw.

I can imagine some commercial breeders smiling or even making fun of such homemade equipment, but they are fun to make, and they can save money. Of course, you have to know what you're doing or you can hurt your birds badly by providing them with makeshift equipment; many cockie owners feel that it doesn't make much sense to buy comparatively expensive birds like cockatiels and then try to save a couple of cents on equipment.

After raising these little tykes by hand from pinfeather stage for the express purpose of filling a special place in the heart and home of a bird lover, I'd far rather earn the price I received again and again by writing and advising than to have the poor little bird I have worked hard over neglected and unhappy because the new owner has had no experience and does not know what to do. When they leave me, they should be the most satisfactory of all pets, and if not, it is the new owner's failure somehow, mostly through lack of experience.

The nest box should be fairly large, for at times both parents like to set in the box, especially when hatching; one

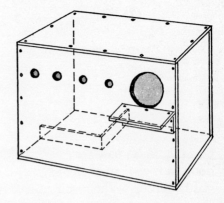

Construction of a nest box
as described by the author.

sets on the eggs and one on the new babies. Because the babies stay in the box until nearly as large as the parents, it is easy to see that a box cannot be too small, as sometimes there are three to seven babies.

I make my nest boxes ten by fifteen by ten inches high for good breathing space. I even put a row of one-half inch holes across the front, near the top, when I build of wood. I do not make saucer-like bottoms, but do make a little L-shaped frame of heavy-weight wooden strips nailed together. I set this in the corner farthest from the door and they use it for the nest. Before I learned to do this I lost several babies by having them wander away from the mother when she could not leave her unhatched eggs; they would stand in a corner of the big box and get chilled. When they grow too crowded in the little nest, I lift the frame out and give them the whole box. I also find cardboard nest boxes very satisfactory. They like them, although they usually chew them up after one or two nestings.

In their little nest frame I have used sand, sawdust, hay chaff, paper torn up fine, wheat bran, lawn clippings and straw. They don't seem to care which, so long as it is there when they choose the box, but I like fine shavings best. In cardboard boxes I lay an old magazine on the bottom and they chew a fine nest out of it. You must use care in removing it later, for they might have chewed through the cardboard also, and the eggs will drop out.

Another view of Kurt feeding from his trophy for the best large foreign cage bird.

I found they like a little front porch just under their door where they can sit to guard the nest, so now they all have a porch with an extra strip nailed across the front edge which they can grasp easily when alighting. Here they sit and survey their world and give all others to understand: this is our house, interfere at your own risk!

When it is about time to lay, the hen especially will be at the grit tray half the time. As she lays every other day, or about every eighteen or twenty hours, I remove the eggs carefully, as she lays them, and replace each one with a china egg or an infertile one from a former nest. (I always save these for patching an egg that might get a little hole in it. I cut a piece of the old egg quite a bit larger than the hole and press it over the hole.) It makes them hatch more evenly if the first three or four eggs are replaced in this way and then set all at once. However, on a nest of three or four eggs or with flighty parents this is *not necessary*.

They are good feeders and devoted parents; when babies are not fed it is not their fault but yours. The only reason a baby does not eat is that it can't eat because of some digestive trouble. When all is well, they are stuffed until the craw is large and distended. You might have heard the old saying "like a bed-tick tied in the middle," and that is a fine description of a well-fed baby cockie.

When doing well, baby cockatiels grow like weeds and look soft, tender, and "juicy." If the craw is not big and soft, but full of hard packed seeds and the baby has a dried-up appearance, its pinfeathers flat and its nostrils extra high and large, or if the eyes don't open on time (six or seven days), there is trouble ahead, most likely serious; so be watchful. This is where tame parents are valuable, since they don't mind your interference.

Know your birds as individuals and watch them for any slight signs of illness; an ounce of prevention is worth pounds of cure here. If anything seems to indicate trouble, check droppings as a further clue and, if necessary, confine the sick bird to a hospital cage for a while for observation.

FEEDING FOR REPRODUCTION. . .

For breeding success, let's say that if birds are of the right age and the season is right, you can get them in condition with full flight and good food. They should be taught to eat lots of greens—not once in a while, when you happen to think of it, or once or twice a week, but every day, as regularly as seed and water. Don't say, "They won't eat it," but *teach* them by providing it constantly. It is a sure thing they can't eat it if it is not given to them. Almost any kind will do. I consider dandelion, celery, carrot, endive, or chickory the best. Lettuce is fine if from field or garden, but it must be watched carefully in the north, as it may be hothouse grown and smoked with nicotine. If this is cut and fed before the ground has had time to absorb the poison, it could kill your whole flock in an hour. Always remember the outside green portions are better than the bleached parts.

Then, feed a good seed mixture, one-half canary, one-half millet (white, yellow, proso, or a mixture of all three). Unless you get plenty of condition oil into the birds, this seed should have on it one teaspoonful of oil to one quart of seed. They need cod-liver oil even in sunny climates. As for sunflower seeds, I prefer the medium or small size to the giant. Birds must have plenty of grit, some good plain dirt and a piece of sod or plaster board.

Now, if they have not been used to soft food, start at once to teach them by giving it every day. Some are very stubborn. I have even had to make them eat it by withholding seed at first. They must learn to use this before babies come or they will not have the proper baby food. If they feed too much hard seed, the babies will not grow, but will become constipated, sick, shrivel up and die. In their native habitat, they follow up the seasons by using milk-stage seeds of the grain and grasses there. So they have with the green foods a nicely balanced semi-soft diet to feed their babies. They do not need to use last year's old, hard, dry seed, such as we have to offer. Since I can't furnish enough milk-stage seeds for them, I make up for it by supplying lots of whole wheat bread.

I dry the bread first; then it keeps indefinitely. When ready to use, I soak it just quickly in water and squeeze as dry as possible so that it makes a nice crumbly food instead of a mush. Since the condition oil will not mix well on bread, I use one-half cup of oil to a one and one-half pound box of cornmeal (yellow), to which is added two tablespoonfuls of bone phosphate and one of iodized salt, and sometimes a teaspoonful of sulphur. Any other dry feeding supplement you might be partial to could also be added.

This oily cornmeal keeps a week or two and is sprinkled over the damp, crumbled bread, as if you were salting something *very heavily*. The condition oil used is three-fourths cod-liver oil and one-fourth wheat germ oil. A little vitamin A oil could be added, though I now use it as vitamin drops in water or mush for the babies only. They might not like the smell or taste of the cod-liver oil at first, but you can give plain bread for a while and then increase oiled meal as tolerated. They soon learn to love it and use it to replace the soft unripe seeds we cannot easily supply. It takes a lot of food to feed a nest of babies, as you will learn if you have to feed a bunch of babies. Plentifully supply their fresh soft food, greens and seed so they do not have to hunt too hard among the hulls for it when they are babies. This is more important for cockies than parrots or some others, because cockatiels are not, as a rule, great fruit eaters. A little apple, sometimes, is about the only fruit I can get them to eat. They dearly love fresh green corn and can be taught to eat peas, fresh or frozen (these to be thawed, but uncooked). Both of these vegetables are comparable to milk-stage seeds.

Mrs. Moon feeding some of her young cockies with food dispensed from a cake decorator. A couple of the older birds are perched on her head and shoulder.

GENERAL FEEDING. . .

I prefer the cafeteria style of feeding, as I have so many birds. Papers are spread on top of a long cage (five by two), and two large trays serve as their table. One tray holds the seed pan and bread dish. This tray catches the seed and feed the birds throw out as they paddle back and forth through it with their big clumsy feet. I give them the regular mixed diet seed, two parts canary, or I use one-half canary and one-half millet. I also offer one dish each of canary and millet separately for those that prefer it.

Into the other tray is emptied all the smaller amounts of seed left in their dishes when I come to refill. The cockatiel's wings, as they alight, blow off the hulls somewhat, and they, as well as a few loose parrakeets and a lot of zebra finches and rice birds, will pick it over when it is spread out thin. The next day it is put on the porch for the doves and quail to pick at and when finally swept up is spread on the garden for the wild birds. During the cold snowy days, however, I put it outside before it is picked over so well, for ordinarily there is very little left for the wild birds. But I pour it out lavishly at first, as the cockies are most important, and then I pass it on until it is all consumed. Even the crumbs and crusts from their bread dish are saved, ground up fine and fed to the meal worms, which in turn the finches and canaries and even some of the 'keets and cockies so dearly love to eat.

At the other end of the table are the greens and any other treat I wish to give them—an apple or carrot stuck on a nail in a block of wood held solidly so they can pick at it, the rinds of juiced oranges which some love to clean out, a pan of sunflower seeds, salted popped corn, a few peanuts, or a dish of oats and carrots cooked together and one of plain hulled oats. These are for a treat and a change.

A shelf away from the food tray holds their water and nothing else, and there's an open dish for bathing if they wish. They do enjoy a bath when setting on dirty, hot little babies. At least once a month their water has a teaspoon of Sal Hepatica, Eno, or Epsom salts (preferred in order named) added to each quart. It won't hurt for several days in succession, or a half day each day for a while.

On another shelf is the grit tray. Don't forget that grit is as important as food; I sprinkle fresh grit over the tray every few days so the birds can pick what they like best and need most.

On the grit tray is fastened a "salt spool." Made for rabbits, this is very hard; when I see the birds working too hard to get some salt, I either soak it, break some off, or set a little dish of mineral food on the tray, to which I add a good pinch of iodized salt. They need and crave salt just as pigeons do, so I keep plenty around, as well as charcoal. In parts of the country where there is no iodine in the soil, it is wise to use iodized salt. A little dish of iodized salt and calcium, half and half, is good.

There is also a dish of plain mineral food and a piece of plaster or plaster board and a piece of cuttlebone. These are wired on the cage so they are solid for them to chew on. When you see a breeding pair, and especially the hen, at the grit tray almost continually, you can soon expect eggs.

GRASSES. . .

In the summer I bring in armloads of grasses and weeds with seed and flowers on them: marigolds, dandelions, plantain, lambsquarter, foxtail tassels which are like tiny millet (their favorite seed)—and other seeding grasses, even the tiny seeds on tickle grass and blue grass. They like to chew the juicy stems of these greens and will work on them for hours.

To me, a beautiful sight is to see the cockatiels on a pile of grasses, with tiny gray and white zebra finches skipping around them either eating or pulling and dragging to get some of it to their nests. Some like tomatoes, and others enjoy three or four meal worms from my fingers when I feed the finches. A special treat is a fresh roasting ear of corn—raw or cooked or the lightly salted cobs left over from your dinner.

EGG FOOD. . .

Egg food should be handled very carefully and kept in a separate dish, lest pieces be dragged out and lost and then picked up later when spoiled, which will cause poisoning. I dislike egg for this reason, but so far I have found nothing to take its place and they love it, so I give it to them and am extra careful. Don't make up too much at a time and do not put grated carrot in it. Not making up too much is especially important if the bread used is already old; the dampness from the egg, and keeping it too long, could be a source of mold, and that is very, very dangerous, causing much suffering and loss of the babies. The egg can be mashed up and fed plain or mixed with a little baby cereal. This should not take the place of the damp bread but is used as a supplement.

TO DETERMINE SEX. . .

There is absolutely no sure way of deciding the sex of a cockie before the head begins to get its color. They all look alike until the head feathers turn, but from much experience, I can usually pick the males in a nest before they are four weeks old. The earlier you can pick the ones you think are males, the more you can check to be sure. When I hear that tiny squeak of a song, I put a dot of Mercurochrome on the head, then I check and recheck. I have made mistakes, but I have had fair luck in guessing correctly. Each "new way" I hear about I test and discard, so don't let anyone fool you by saying that males have more red or yellow, few dots, etc. Song, actions and yellow throat are the only characteristics.

I also band each nest of young birds so I will know which nest they belong to, and can, by comparison with each other, decide which are the males much earlier. I find that in a full breeding season the babies run about half males and half hens. Sometimes an egg or two is broken or doesn't hatch and the ones that do hatch are males, which leads some breeders to think they will raise so many more males, but with the hundreds I have raised, I believe fifty-fifty is a fair average over the entire season.

TO HAND FEED. . .

When the little fellows are quite covered with their long "porcupine" quills, but before these quills begin to fluff out into feathers, I slip them away from the nest one at a time, every few days, and train them to hand feeding. It is easier for me and for the parents that way. When one baby learns to eat well on being hand fed, his "squealing" helps to teach the others. I take the baby away in the mid-afternoon and seldom try to feed until the next morning, when it is hungry and usually takes the food without any trouble.

A baby of this age is about the limit for easy hand feeding. If any older, they are as stubborn to teach to eat out of a feeder as a calf to eat out of a bucket. If they have not been handled before flying out of their box, it is ten times more work, and there is much less chance of success in taming them. The younger and smaller they are, the more readily they will take to hand feeding and the easier to tame. But, of course, it *is* more work, for when they are very young feeding must be every hour; when larger, every two or three hours, or whenever the crop feels empty. Always remember —little and often is the safest rule.

But with regular feedings and a drink of water (one or two dropperfuls) in between feedings, once or twice a day, they surely keep you busy. Unless you are a real bird lover, you are very likely to do as a Virginia lady did after raising three—give up! She wrote that she would race through her housework and watch the clock and then gag over having to chew up the food. She sent her Becky back to me as a gift, and I have enjoyed helping little Becky to raise her babies.

Chewing their food for them never bothers me. Either I am more of a bird lover than most people or I have an extra good stomach, perhaps both. When I have an "only" of one age, rather than use the feeder, I take a spoonful of food as I go by, chew it until warm and grab up the little scamp and feed him directly from my mouth with barely a break in my other work. But when I have anywhere from six to eighteen youngsters, I warm the food over a pan of hot water and use the feeder. They must *never* be fed cold food. This can upset their digestion in one feeding.

FEEDERS. . .

A glass tube canary feeder is satisfactory for young birds. If you are feeding quite a few babies, such a tube would be too small. One baby will take three-fourths of a tubeful soon after he learns to eat. Don't ever keep on feeding until he stops squawking or you will kill him. They don't know when they have had enough. If they won't quit squealing for food when I know they are full, I gave a dropperful of water.

I've tried, without success, to find or have made a larger feeder, so I devised mine out of an aluminum plunger-type cake decorator (somewhat like an auto grease gun) replacing the short blunt nose with an oil can spout. It works very well, and they soon squeal with delight whenever they see it. Of course, they get the mush all over themselves and each other, but when weaned they clean themselves up. If they don't, a good bath in a mild suds and several rinsings and a roll up for an hour or so in an old wool sweater or piece of blanket makes them soft as silk again.

I had to experiment on my first birds to get the proper formula for their feedings, and while I have used various other mixtures since, none has ever worked any better. The base I use is a quick-cook rolled oats. I add a little powdered or canned milk. Use any good dry nestling food to bring this mixture to the right consistency. For those first three precious little fellows, I chewed up the dry food—took a bite of gruel and chewed them together—until fine and warm. I think the saliva helped also and it is always the same temperature. It worked fine on my three K's.

You can also use any of the light flaky ready-cooked baby cereals instead of oats. I use them when I am in a hurry or when the oats are not cooked ahead, for a meal or two, but it is more costly and the oats work much better in a big feeder. It is not necessary to put the oats through a sieve when the birds are three or four weeks old.

One of the most valuable additions I have made to the formula is to add boiled carrots, pressed through a sieve, to the gruel (be sure and add the water they are boiled in to the cooked oats). I owe thanks for this to Dr. Knapp of Ohio State University, to whom I sent the body of a baby that died and a couple of live babies so that he might observe and examine them. He said they showed a lack of vitamin A, and carrot is a good source of it. Another very easy recipe is: soak four slices of whole wheat bread in hot water until it is very soft. Squeeze the bread out and add two teaspoonsful of powdered milk, three-fourths teaspoonful of plain gelatine, one-fourth teaspoonful bone phosphate, any good baby vitamin drops (containing A, B, C, D, E), a little canned baby food, and greens or carrots. You can use this for one or two feedings daily.

A sand and gravel mixture is good for lining the bottom tray of a cage. However, a separate dish of grit should be given. This is an indispensable item, especially for hens during breeding time.

MILLET. . .

There is on the market now peeled millet, which is invaluable for hand feeding. It may be ground while the birds are small, and later added whole to their mush, if you have a large hole in the feeder—it won't come through a glass canary feeder. You can also add bone charcoal, which is better than ordinary charcoal for hand feeding. If you have no proper feeder and can't make one, your baby birds can be taught to eat out of a teaspoon, letting them bite on the edge of the spoon, but the feeder is much easier. When you feed whole millet, a tiny pinch of grit should be added to *one* feeding every other day. Use care that they don't get too much grit.

DROPPINGS. . .

Watch the droppings. They are naturally looser when the babies are hand-fed, because more soft food is used. Yet the droppings should have some form to them, and they should have color according to what is being fed. If the droppings are too watery or quite green, the diet may not be just right, or it could be caused by a cold, a damp box, or from some other reason. If a cold is noticed, give (a half teaspoonful to a pint of water) Sal Hepatica. This will usually work it off. If not, use a sulfathiazole.

Cockatiels can be taught to stand on one's shoulder. This is made easier by wearing clothes which the bird can cling onto, for instance sweaters. Jerky movements should be avoided so as not to startle it.

It is also a good idea to keep all their water well pinked up with some good germ-killing preparation. I use one in all the water I feed them between meals. It will help guard against digestive upsets. Then, if some morning their appetites seem off, I give one dropper of Eno or Sal Hepatica (one-half teaspoonful to a pint of water) before any breakfast is given, and give smaller meals for a while. It must be remembered, however, that baby birds never take as much food in the mornings or seem as ravenous as during the late afternoons when nature calls for a big fill-up for the night.

For the well-balanced diet that I have worked out through much experience, the cooked oats, carrot, nestling foods, and peeled millet (used sparingly) make a diet always easy to get and perfect enough to raise many a fine healthy bird.

TAMING. . .

Hand feeding is the easiest way to make the finest tame birds—*if* you have the patience, time, and the knack of such handling. By weaning time the babies will have lost all fear of your hands; they will know your voice and love the sight of you. They forget their parents and look to you for everything. Of course, if after taming they are put off in a cage away from you and never handled or talked to, they will not stay tame, and your previous work will have been all for nothing. They must always be kept near you, on you, petted and loved. They dislike a small cage and feel free and happy when out of it.

I trim all wings, so for their exercise they hold on to me with strong little claws and flap their wings. I lift and pet and handle each one every chance I get. When they are sitting on top of the cage I stop and pet and lift each one as I go by. And as soon as they are able, I begin to make them "step up" on my hand—a fine approach for later on. They are soon glad to do this when they fly to the floor and "want up," so for training I do not pick them up but pass my hand right over their feet until it touches the legs or breast, and they step up at once.

However, if for any reason they cannot be hand fed, I

use another method of taming them. I pet and talk to them as many times a day from the time they come out of the shell. When they begin to hiss and scold at me, which they do even before their eyes are open at six or seven days, I keep it up until they calm down. In the second and third weeks I begin taking them out of the box—leaving one or two in each time so as not to worry the parents. I set them in a shallow pan, dish, or box several times a day. This gives them a chance to look around to see me and get used to noises and movements. I imagine I look quite different, when seen as a whole person, compared to just the bit of hands or face they have been seeing from down in the dark nest box. It is no wonder they are sometimes frightened. Some run backwards like a crawfish and almost as fast, until they fall off on the floor if not watched; more pitiful are the ones that just sit still and cry.

Now is the time to really talk to them, so they learn the comfort of your voice. As soon as they can cling to your shoulders, they must learn to ride there. If I'm wearing a starched dress it is hard for them to hold on, so I throw an old turkish towel or a cape of some soft, rough material around me, or put on a sweater—which also helps keep the starched dress more presentable. You'll have to do a bit of training on yourself also and learn not to walk stiffly and uncomfortably, or it will be such hard work you'll be tempted to give up, or at least not do it enough to do the job well.

I'm so used to the feel of birds on my head and shoulders I miss them when they are not there. Of course, I have to be careful of a new nest of weanlings, as any sudden noise will make them crawfish; then, quicker than a wink, they drop to the floor. But they soon learn to know I'm their best friend in the big outside world and to cling tight while I go about any and every chore of bird room or housework, just as though I were not taming cockies to make some home happier.

WEANING. . .

The weaning of hand fed tame babies is no trick at all. Just begin by putting them in a cage or on top of one, as you like, when they have outgrown their nursery box. Put seed and water there for them to pick at; feed their mush out of a

Diagram of flight feathers, showing feathers clipped to hinder flight.

dish instead of their bottle, but always offer the bottle for their final meal of the day, lest one or two do not get enough.

Always feel each little tummy before putting the cockie to bed. If it is not full, fill it somehow, by dish, bottle, or by mouth, but be sure none goes through the night on an empty crop or he'll be going downhill soon. Later, keep less soft mush and more egg food and bread and milk in the regular diet.

It is much harder to tame the bird and yet let the parents feed off, but it can be done. These birds are usually not as tame as hand fed ones, because you will seldom work at the taming. You'll let any number of chances slip by when busy or going away or this and that. You know that the parents are feeding them, so you think you'll start training the next time, and soon the little fellows are growing up and don't know or like you very well.

One simple way of taming I use is to put them in a nursery cage, which is a fifteen by fifteen parrot cage set in a large suit box to catch the seed. I hang a long, low pan on the outside of the parrot cage; they put their little heads through the bars to eat (when the parents come in and out of the cage a few times it shows them how). Also a little seed must be scattered on the floor. The outside dish saves a lot of waste, for at first they do more paddling through it with their clumsy big feet than eating. I carry this cage with me as much as possible, keeping it out of sight or hearing of the parents, except for feeding four or five times a day, and then I allow the parents to come into the cage—and how they do stuff the little rascals through the bars! The main thing is to keep the parents away as much as possible, while I keep the babies with me and handle them all I can.

While I wash dishes or work in the kitchen they are set in a window nearby; if sewing, on a chair at my side. Usually I take them out of the nest at two and one-half or three weeks and out for good at three and one-half or four weeks. At five or six weeks they are eating fairly well alone and the parents feed them only once or twice a day.

At eight or ten weeks they are ready to go to new homes, although most of them are kept longer, depending on the weather and the length of the trip, etc. When a little niece of mine moved away from her grandmother to another state, she described her homesickness as "feeling sick" way down in the bottom of her stomach. When my birds go, I really do feel homesick for several days, or until at least I hear of their safe arrival and that they are loved. Shame on those few who never even once write me this news that I wait for so anxiously!

After your little bird comes, love and handle it a lot. Others resent the strange owner, home, cage, and all, and have a plain case of homesickness. If your bird takes this attitude, leave him more or less alone for a few days, but not too long. When he flies back to his cage continuously, take him to another room or remove the cage so he can't see it. I prefer to cut the wing flight feathers. Some think this is almost a crime, but many a bird has been saved by having its wings cut; full wings can cost the loss of your pet very easily.

Your sick bird

Cockatiels are usually hardy, but close confinement (which is unnatural to birds) and wrong feeding often cause trouble. I have worked with the departments of veterinary science at universities to gather sick or dead birds from everyone for a number of years. I have had many letters about cockatiel troubles and many questions as to Why This and Why That. I've had illnesses strike my own birds and I have had losses, so all in all I do think I have learned a few things about bird illnesses that would have been worth a lot to me if I could have laid my hands on the information when I first needed it.

I have studied poultry books for help, and I corresponded with Robert Stroud (the Birdman of Alcatraz) before I got his book *Stroud's Digest on the Diseases of Birds*, published by T.F.H. Publications. Although he said he could give me no definite experience with cockatiels, his experiences with other birds were valuable, and his book described uremic poisoning so well that when it hit my Buzzie I was able to diagnose it at once; the remedy Mr. Stroud gave, coupled with the most attentive care I ever gave any bird, saved Buzzie's life.

I knew Buzzie was a little run-down, thin from quarreling with another bird, and not eating right. When he did not come to me as usual one morning, I put him in a cage and watched for droppings. An east wind had blown in that night, and while several birds were in a row on a perch, it got him because of his run-down condition. None of the others got sick, but poor Buzzie was terribly ill.

I kept a record of all I did for him and just how he

*A much newer comprehensive book about the diseases of birds is *Bird Diseases*, by L. Arnall and I.F. Keymer; this book, also published by T.F.H. Publications, is comparatively expensive but immensely authoritative and useful.

A male cockatiel in perfect form. Eyes that are alert, a raised crest, smooth feathers, and an over-all sleek appearance indicate that a bird is very healthy. Photo courtesy of Heat-X Company.

acted. I never let myself hope for his life for fully ten days. He was so weak he lay on his side; one leg and one wing drooped helplessly, and he had convulsions every little while. During the worst of the illness I stayed with him almost all night, or got up several times during the night. I kept him under an aquarium light bulb in a box.

There were absolutely no droppings for a while. After a dose or two of Sal Hepatica (one-half teaspoonful to one pint of water—my first remedy for almost everything), I started in on the diuretic; soon there were tiny droppings and after a while a wet ring around them. I also gave him a few doses of sulfathiazole and offered food every little while as soon as the wet spots appeared. Before this I feared to force any food, but after his kidneys and bowels began to function I'd put a few drops of nourishing food down to keep his strength and was greatly encouraged when he took a little voluntarily.

An authority at a university, when he read my diary of

this illness, declared it was pneumonia, but I still believe and agree with Robert Stroud that nephritis and uremic poisoning are far more prevalent than pneumonia. I have read about them both, and I never throw a bird away. I try different treatments on it, until better or dead, and then all are opened and studied after they die. The lungs show plainly if it is pneumonia.

You may say, "I thought you loved your birds more than that," but if I can learn anything from one of the pets I have lost to help save my others, or the one you have, I think that is really loving them. It pays to study some of these things ahead of time. Often the bird is dead before the inexperienced owner can diagnose the trouble or even realize the bird is sick. The little fellow will perk up at the approach of his master and keep him from realizing how sick the cockie really is. Uremic poisoning is usually met with in adult birds.

The questions I most often get are: Why are the eggs not fertile? Why don't the parents set? Why don't they feed their babies? Well, I feed plenty of egg food with the oils on it and have recently discovered that the finest natural source of vitamin B is a defatted wheat germ. We use it on all our own cereals and some goes in all bird foods. It can be purchased in pet shops.

Wheat-germ oil, the oil completely separated from the granulated meal, keeps perfectly without getting rancid. These two products should take care of infertile eggs. The wheat-germ meal supplies proteins and vitamin B, which promotes better appetite so that the birds consume enough food to make them fit to lay and rear. I think vitamin B is woefully lacking in most of our foods.

Birds don't refuse to set because they are sick, but mostly because of lack of exercise to digest the heavy rich food they need to make the eggs. I've never had a parent bird or a single egg-bound hen leave the nest since I have given them freedom of the room and fed them as I have advised.

As to raising babies to the size of a little chicken, then deserting them as so many say they do, that I do not believe is ever actually the case. The truth is that the little birds are sick and cannot eat, or they take so little food that the par-

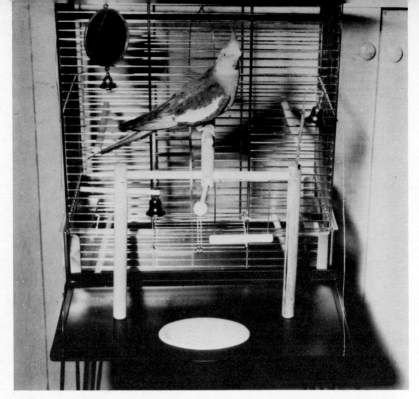

Shown is a cage constructed especially for cockatiels. It includes an outside perch, several bells, a mirror, and a small bathing dish. Photo by Louise Van der Meid.

ents get discouraged trying. Sometimes you can take these babies and hand feed them and get them through. Some complain that they "go light" (lose weight) at about the time for leaving the nest. It is all about the same thing. I am convinced *wrong diet* is to blame. They don't have enough surplus vitamins to withstand any extra drain. Whenever something lessens their intake of nourishment, they go downhill rapidly and are soon dead—if not taken in hand at once. I immediately start to hand feed.

Another factor is *sore mouths* so they can't eat. For this I swab the mouth with a mouthwash antiseptic. I believe this to be an acid condition from some unbalanced diet. Cremo carbonates, a thick white liquid, is very good to counteract this. It coats the whole digestive tract and relieves irritation and inflammation.

If they can't eat, they must be force-fed until they can. I've had babies that were force-fed for quite a while and barely held their own, then all at once they started to gobble food as if starved and gained until fat as pigs. More often the sore mouth goes on down to the crop; the lining of the crop gets thick and inflamed, and then they can't digest or handle the food. I've had to empty and wash out little crops several times, feeding light nestling food with carrot juice instead of milk. If you feed it fairly thin and very warm, little and often, they usually recover. This is the hardest thing to conquer, for sometimes they throw up everything you put down.

Some think this is a mold. Frankly, I don't know what it is. I've found Listerine (pure) and Sterisan solution both good. Sterisan is quite concentrated and must be diluted carefully. This treatment often stops the problem if used at once, so I check every day. If not stopped, it goes down into the craw and hinders or stops digestion, or even goes into the bronchial tubes. Either will cause death.

Your bird should not always be confined in a cage, especially if the cage is not very large. Just like any other animal, birds too need some exercise. This was Snowflake, son of Moonbeam. Photo by Frances Holland.

THE WONDER DRUGS — PENICILLIN, CHLOROMYCETIN, AUREOMYCIN, TERRAMYCIN. . .

I have used penicillin with good results, not to cure sour mouth but to counteract the poison. Penicillin is best for counteracting poisons and respiratory troubles; it will not help a virus. Penicillin is available in inexpensive little 50,000-unit soluble tablets, sealed in squares of tinfoil. A bird can take this much for five to seven days if necessary. I also give shots of penicillin in oil, one-fourth cc. for cockies, one-half to five-eights cc. for parrots. However, I've had the most surprising results from parrakeets and finches, because it seems that most of their troubles, except dietary, are viruses. Many a little parrakeet or finch which I had no hope of saving was as good as new after five to six days of chloromycetin in the drinking water. I use one capsule (one hundred milligrams) to three ounces of water for small birds. For a cockie I put a smaller capsule (fifty milligrams) right down whole or divide it into two doses. A small bird should have at least fifty milligrams a day; some can take one hundred milligrams. A bird the size of a parrot must have two hundred to two hundred and fifty milligrams. It should be used for five or six days.

Only once have I known it to make a bird sick. When I gave two hundred and fifty milligrams to Rita, a big red macaw, he threw up and was desperately ill. I decided to give three to eight drops Cremo carbonates three hours apart, then a hundred-milligram dose of chloromycetin twice a day; this was tolerated. He is a fine bird today, but at that time he was so sick that he couldn't eat, lost flesh, and passed blood.

Some people say not to feed the birds during the time these drugs are given, but I have found they are much more likely to make the birds sick if they are given on an empty stomach. So feed the bird first, if only a little bit.

Some birds, like some humans, are allergic to these antibiotics. It is a good plan to give half the dose and wait to see the reaction, giving the rest later. Some cockies take one-quarter cc. penicillin well, but others will almost pass out from the same dose.

In addition to having a slighter build, female cockatiels lack the lemon yellow face and throat and black underfeathers on the tail which the males have.

Undesirable deposits of crystallized materials can also be found in the crop like this one taken from a parrakeet. Photo by Dr. L. Arnall.

There is also a water-soluble sulfathiazole which is fine for treating colds. I follow the directions on the package for chickens and give in drinking water or by dropper.

HARD CROP. . .

I have owned two males that are such hard workers,that they pack their babies with seed until the crops are hard and cannot digest. One of these birds will stuff seven to ten parrakeéts and raise them all right and then kill his own three or four babies with kindness. I try to induce him to use more soft food and greens, and maybe I change to fresh grit; available salt may make them consume more water. I add vitamin B to food or water. There are small tablets, powder, or liquid. Three or four drops can be given directly in the mouth or put in food or water. There is not much danger of giving too much, as the body throws off the excess.

If I think the crop is packed too hard, especially if it is still hard in the morning, I give a dropper of water with Sal Hepatica or Eno salts   (one-half teaspoon to one pint of water), then in two hours I give about three drops of mineral oil. If this doesn't help, I wash out the crop, give two or three drops of Cremo carbonates, a dropper of water, and hand-feed on a soft no-seed diet.

I often give the parents the same salts and water to

drink. In fact, it is a good habit to give this water every week or so for a day or two to all birds; it wards off ills by cleaning them out. I was told the oldest canary I ever heard of—twenty-four years old—had this water one day each week all his life. If you can't hand feed, I would take all small seed from the parents and give sunflower seeds, soft feed, lots of greens and apple and the salts and water.

LAMENESS. . .

I have had three or four lame birds and have heard of many birds suddenly going lame with a hot feverish swollen foot. Again I try to induce the parents to eat more greens and salts in water. I give the little one four to five dropperfuls of this water a day for several days. I paint the foot with iodine after a ten-minute soak in hot (not *too* hot) water. This lameness comes on at two or three months of age. Two cockies I sold as "lame birds" and two that I kept cleared up shortly. I saw one of the birds I sold later and he was fine—a lovely bird. I never heard about the other one. The feeding of bone phosphates or calcium helps lameness.

Another kind of lameness occurs when the baby is only a week or so old. The little fellow will chew at the joint where feathers and bare leg meet; the leg swells and gets sore. I give them the same treatment and all but one I did not notice in time has recovered nicely. The bone in the leg seemed to be injured, and when I treated it it appeared to clear up, but later the little foot was twisted over to one side as though it had been broken. He is lovely and cute but walks on the side of his foot and limps. In addition to the outward treatment, I give the bird one drop a day of (concentrated) multiple vitamins, for this weakness can be caused by a vitamin deficiency.

COLDS. . .

Birds take cold just as humans do. They get runny noses, swollen eyes and throats too sore to swallow. They cough and sneeze from a cold just as we do and they need the same treatment—warmth, salts in water, and quiet. If you have a pet remedy for yourself and your family, weaken it one-

A lesser sulphur-crested cockatoo measures about 33 cm. long and is only a little bit more than half the length of its bigger relative, the greater sulphur-crested cockatoo. Photo by Horst Mueller.

The pileated parrakeet is a very colorful bird that is rarely seen in this country. Photo by Horst Mueller.

A trio of Chinese button quails. The bird in the center is a female. Males are more colorful than the females. Photo by Horst Mueller.

Left: Leadbeater's cockatoo is a very beautiful bird. Right: rose-breasted cockatoo, also known as roseate cockatoo. Photos by Horst Mueller.

fourth or one-half and use it for your bird.

I use ST-37, peroxide, and mouth washes undiluted for swabbing sore throats. Use a little of any good nose drops. Isedrin is fine—one drop to each nostril. Argyrol is my old standby. Dropped in the eyes it runs all through the sinuses and into the mouth and throat. I never use over a ten percent solution, but I believe five percent is too weak. It loses strength, so keep the solution fresh.

Soluble sulfathiazole in drinking water for five days is fine, and to build up resistance use daily a drop of concentrated vitamin A and D your pet shop offers. Read the label and compare units so that you will purchase the best.

Tame cockies are trusting and will not hesitate to sit on their owner's hand, shoulder, or head. Photo by M.E. Ginaven.

SORE EYES. . .

Colds often cause sore eyes. A cockie was just recently brought here to board. He must have caught cold on the way; he seemed all right when he arrived except that I noticed immediately that his droppings were thin and bright green. The next day one eye was swollen shut.

I used ten percent Argyrol and dropped it in his eyes twice daily and applied a little yellow oxide of mercury once daily. Yellow oxide of mercury was personally recommended to me by Robert Stroud several years ago. The bird was a pitiful sight, as Argyrol stains like iodine, but his mistress was gone two and a half months, so he was all cleaned up before she got back, even if I did have my own fingers to doctor every time I doctored him. A saturated solution of sodium perborate is also good, and doesn't stain. To make it put in water and pour off the clear portion for use. It will keep. Your pet shop has antibiotic salves that are wonderful helps.

SORE SPOTS. . .

I've never had one of my birds pick a bare spot on himself, but I have heard of any number of them doing it. I had one brought here and I fed him with my birds for four months to see if a change of diet helped, but there was no improvement and he was taken home before I could experiment further with him.

It still seems to me to be caused by a lack in the diet and if I had one I would give the usual salts in water for three or four weeks. I would put Merthiolate with five percent salicylic acid on the skin followed by sulphur and lard ointment, used sparingly—the birds don't like to be greasy. Work in all the sulphur you can, still leaving it soft enough to spread. I think vitamin B is well worth trying. Of course, the oils and wheat germ, already mentioned, used as a part of his diet might help. To cover more than one-third of the body at once with anything greasy induces pneumonia and is very dangerous.

I had a bird brought to me who had picked himself raw; in six months he grew lovely new plumage with my regular

Some varieties of parrakeets: albino, greens, cobalt blue, and lutino. Parrakeets can learn to talk extremely well and become very tame. Photo by Horst Mueller.

Lories are very colorful birds that are quite noisy. Chattering lory (left), black capped lory (right). Photos by Horst Mueller.

A pair of Gouldian finches. The male (right) is more brightly colored than the female (left). Photo by Horst Mueller.

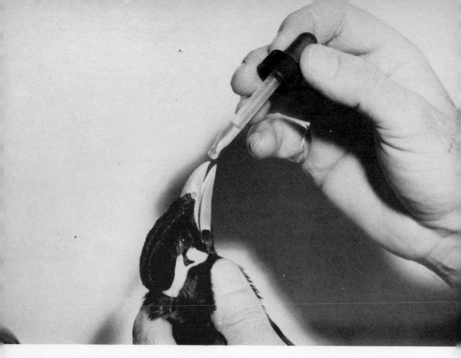

Administering medication by an ordinary eye-dropper is both practical and efficient. This mynah bird is being held in such a way as to immobilize its wings. Photo by Louise Van der Meid.

feeding and care. I used vitamin B and an eczema ointment. He was finally given to me for the six months' board bill and is still lovely, although I expected him to die every day for the first month.

TREATING. . .

If the bird struggles or you are afraid he will bite you, the simplest method is to wrap him in a bath towel, all but the face. Wrap or roll him so the wings and feet are out of the way and so that only the mouth, nose and eyes are visible. This will stop much of the struggling and the chance of the bird's getting away from you; it will also keep you from injuring him in your efforts to hold him still.

If you are giving a pill that is not soluble in water, cut it up small; smooth the sharp edges with a dampened finger and just push the pieces down with a toothpick on which you have rolled cotton. A throat swab can be made of almost any little stick; wet it and roll on a bit of cotton. This covers the sharp edges and makes it safe to use.

If the pill is soluble in water, a dropper is the easy way. Use only a ball-or-bulb-tipped medicine dropper and insert it *way down* in the crop so as not to strangle the bird. A canary can take very little, but a cockie can take a dropperful. If they won't drink, I always give water by medicine dropper. Do not try this with a parrot—he can break the glass. I use a small teaspoon for them, filled only a quarter full, and put it far back on the tongue and let the liquid run down.

To wash out a bird's crop, wrap him up in a towel and put down two or three droppers of warm water with a bit of salt or soda or antiseptic added. If the crop is hard, massage it until it loosens, then hold the bird's head down and empty the crop by massaging toward the mouth. Repeat if necessary until the crop is cleaned out, and then use another dropper of water to stay down and let the bird rest. Use one-half teaspoonful of soda to a cup of water for this last dropperful.

When you are going to attend a sick or injured bird, do not go at it as if you were afraid or he will sense it. Be calm and make every movement count. Don't let a sick bird get away from you and fly about, which does much harm. Wrapping him up in a towel prevents this.

To bathe a sore foot, wrap the bird in a towel and hold the foot under the faucet (only a mixed faucet where the hot and cold water run together and can be tempered). If you do not have a mixed faucet, hold the bird over a cup or small can or jar, keeping the sore foot in the warm water; change the water if necessary to keep it warm. Always keep your own finger by the sore foot in order to gauge the temperature of the water.

Dry the foot before painting it with iodine. It is also good to rub on a tiny bit of salve, after the iodine dries, as iodine seems to dry the skin. Merthiolate should be used if a cut or sore is "open" and followed up with sulfathiazole or penicillin salve to keep out infection. If a cut is not open, I like iodine. *Never, never* tie up or cover iodine, as it will surely blister the skin.

Scarlet macaw. Photo by Horst Mueller.

Blue and gold macaw; macaws in general are large, strong-billed birds and need strong and roomy living quarters. Photo by Horst Mueller.

A hybrid macaw, the result of a cross between a scarlet macaw and a blue and gold macaw. Photo by Ralph Small.

A whimsical photo of cockatiels "having tea." Photo by John Knapp.

I use sulfathiazole powder, soluble in water. I give one-fourth teaspoon to one pint for three to five days. If the bird is too sick to drink much, double the amount for two days, then use as directed above for two to four days more. A little soda (one-half teaspoon to one pint of water) makes this drug easier on the kidneys. A dropper half full of the stronger solution may be given four to six times a day to relieve respiratory troubles. Dissolve one 50,000 unit water-soluble tablet of penicillin in six droppers of water and give one-half dropperful every three hours until used up. Repeat for six days if needed. I keep it in the refrigerator, although some say this is not necessary. I use crystalline penicillin G potassium (soluble). These two drugs are wonderful for any infection, while the aureomycin is best for virus diseases. Terramycin is better still, for it seems to be tolerated more easily. These two drugs come in capsules, and a cockie can take a fifty milligram capsule every day for five days. The next two days give one-half this dose. I have given two capsules a day for the first three days in severe cases.

Koxy grown up—
beautiful lady

As a baby Koxy was a sassy little thing, and she is still as independent as they come. If she were human I think she would be called a typical "old maid." She will ride on my shoulder half a day at a time yet does not care to be petted or made a lot of by anyone. She shows a great preference for me and loves to have me clap my hands at her, and then she will jump and flap her wings. She made up to her brother Kurt from the very first. They were good companions, and when they were old enough they wanted a box together, but I had brought her a mate of unrelated blood and brought a hen for Kurt. I caged them for a while with their new mates.

Kurt and his mate started to work at once, but Koxy pouted for three or four months before she would accept a box her King had chosen. Then she laid six eggs when fourteen months old. The eggs were all fertile, but as I had not learned about nest frames, four of the babies wandered away and were chilled; one I carried to the home of a friend whose birds never had anything but infertile eggs, hoping that feeding a baby might help her birds get started. The last one, Junior, they raised, but Koxy never did like King and only put up with him from necessity.

When it was her turn to go back in the box when setting, instead of slipping in and sitting beside him a while as most do, she would go in, and he would come out as if kicked out. She'd even bite him until he cried out, but they worked together one season and brought fine babies. The next season, he deserted her for Karol—and I can't say I blame him.

Then I got her Kim. She acted about the same with him, but he was such a jealous bird he wanted to claim the whole bird room for his bride, so after that season I sold him. The

Star finches are small but quite attractive.

Except for the yellow color near the beak and around the eye, the hyacinthine macaw is a large bird with rich hyacinth blue plumage. Photo by Horst Mueller.

The yellow-fronted Amazon is just one of the many species of the parrot genus *Amazona* from the Caribbean and South America. Photo by Horst Mueller.

Shown here is Cocky, one of Koxy's first babies. For many Christ-mases he "autographed" Mrs. Moon's greeting cards.

next time she had only an old bird for a mate and lost a sea-son's eggs. The next time it was a young mate, and another season was lost so far as hatching her own eggs. I have given her several eggs from other nests each time to hatch out and raise, for that is her greatest pleasure, and now she is mother-ing four, not her own, and is so happy she doesn't care for a mate. Instead she sits in the box beside the big fat babies and looks so contented and happy I can hardly bear to take them away to hand feed. I may just bring her box in and let her feed them off, as she is so tame we will get along nicely to-gether. If they are where they can see me a lot and I can pet and handle them often, they will be real nice and she'll be happy.

I really expect her to have some of her own next time, as her mate is older now. I think so much of Koxy that I let her go about as she pleases. She will fly in from the bird room, through the living room and into the kitchen to my shoulder so softly that I never know when she is coming until she lands. How she knows I am there is a mystery, because she is around a corner and can't see me until she's a few feet from me. She knows there is a boiled egg in the refrigerator and gives me no peace until I fix it for her. I never censure her for not loving her mates too much, for I took away the only one she really did love, because it was her brother. Koxy has always been so pretty and smooth and never thought enough of her mates to let them pick her baldheaded and bare as most do.

Darling Koxy, the first and the last of the three little K's born February first, 1940, died November twenty-sixth, 1951, just two days before scheduled to go on TV in the interest of the Third National Cage Bird Week. She was not sick; her little heart just seemed worn out with age, just like her daddy's, and the last trip from my shoulder to the feed table was too much. I picked her up, held and loved her ten minutes, and she was gone. I had her loving companionship and sweet memories nearly twelve years.

KURT GROWN UP—ARISTOCRATIC COLONEL. . .

I've seen pictures of such proud aristocratic gentlemen of the long-whiskered period, and Kurt's stately bearing always reminds me of them. If any bird could be said to frown, he surely could—and could follow it up with enforcement, if necessary. He was a good faithful mate to his Karol as long as he lived, and a hard worker for his family. His only bad habit was to strip them of all their feathers except the heavy wing and tail ones. I watched him often. He would eat his fill and go into the box and if a little one did not come up at once he would grab a feather, then he'd yank one out after another. He was in a hurry to get them all filled up, and no wonder, because he had five of his own and two of a neighbor's.

Strawberry finches are very brightly colored birds and are also very good singers. Photo by Louise Van der Meid.

Two colorful representatives of the rosella group: Stanley rosella parrakeet (left), red rosella parrakeet (right). Photos by Horst Mueller.

A white
cockatiel
photographed in
a bird park in
Germany. Photo
by Horst
Mueller.

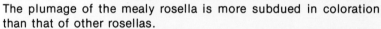

The plumage of the mealy rosella is more subdued in coloration than that of other rosellas.

Kurt gave us and our bird visitors many a laugh. After I brought the seven in for hand feeding, he hunted until he found them, even though I kept the box covered. Then to see him work to get down in the box was a sight. He'd pull and jerk at that cloth, and then he'd try to find a place to crawl under. Finally he would get in, and then the little squealers would give him away and I'd get him out. But he was all business and would start working with great haste again. He did work very hard with that big nest, but the next time he had only one of his own and one of another—his last baby, so I kept my little Kurtlette and was recently more than glad to buy back one of his big boys—the very image of him.

It was very hot weather and Kurt often slept in a window. Because he was perhaps a bit run down from hard work, I think he took cold; even with all my work and worry I could not save him. I supposed it was pneumonia until I got my Stroud book and read how colds can settle in the kidneys. I know I could have saved his life if I had had that information then, plus penicillin and sulfa.

At first I feared something contagious, so I isolated him. He still longed for his Karol, so I finally said I did not care if I lost her too, because he should have her with him until he died. I knew then that he would die, for he never ate a bite or took a drop of water until the last day, when his fever was so high he drank all I would give him. So Karol sat beside him stroking his head feathers until the evening of the twelfth day, and when she went to stay with the babies, I put him to bed in his little box, and in a half hour he was dead—leaving poor Karol and myself to feed the two babies.

Karol was so lost without her Kurt I couldn't take them away entirely. I put them in a box with seven others and whenever she would hear me feeding she'd come in and feed hers. I let her raise her last baby and I took over the other one. Karol is still here and with King as her mate has brought me lots of fine babies which don't get stripped any more.

She has just done a wonderful job—hatched one orphan egg and mothered the baby. Before she finished this she had laid her own eggs. I helped by feeding the little thing three or four times a day, because Karol was not eating just right to

Kurt photographed at the prime of his life.

be feeding a tiny baby and had also started to lay, but she fed him. She was the only cockie on a nest at the time, and none of the 'keets would have him; one nearly killed him when I tried, so between us, Karol and I managed. Yet some people say they never dare look in the box. Well, I would miss half my fun that way. I could have raised this little fellow myself, but I did not feel well enough to take the responsibility.

Spotty and Becky are two of Karol's and King's daughters and are also fine working mothers. Kurtlette also has been bringing me many nice babies ever since she started at seven and one-half months. So some of Kurt's grandchildren are still going out to make other homes happy. I have many happy memories of him and a life-sized picture framed on my wall, so natural that other cockies recognize it as a cockatiel when I hold them up to it. I also have the ribbons and rosettes and beautiful cups he won when he was best of all large foreign birds in the Dayton, Ohio, bird show.

Mynahs make good pets. They can be taught to talk and are very hardy birds.

Both male and female Barnard parrots show the same color pattern, except that the females appear duller, particularly in the reddish part of the forehead. Photo by Horst Mueller.

White Java rice birds are not albinos. This variety first appeared in captive birds as a mutation affecting the loss of pigment in the plumage only. The reddish beaks and legs and dark eyes of the gray or wild form are retained.

KEWPIE AND BUGGLES—TRAGIC ENDINGS. . .

Kewpie was almost everybody's favorite, although I love all my birds and show no partiality. He learned to talk more than Kurt, although I don't think Kurt really tried, and would often say things in a whisper. Kewpie would go to anyone and talk for anyone. He could not bear to have you say good-bye or to put on a hat or coat, which was indeed the cause of his loss.

He wanted to go with my daughter when she left the house and watched his chance when the door opened wide enough. Soon he was up and over the top and out to find her. And as usual, when the surroundings looked strange to him, never having seen the house from the outside, he was frightened and didn't know where to go. If my daughter had still been on the porch, no doubt he would have lit on her, but she was already in the car and he could not find her. So he flew, screaming as he went, and that was the last we ever saw of him. It was on Christmas day and even though it was only a little bird that was lost, it spoiled our day and Christmas dinner. It was very warm for that time of the year and we worried for three weeks about what was happening to him until at last a zero spell came, and then we knew he would be dead.

Buggles was my new Judy's first baby, a little hen, and one of the most loving and sweet-dispositioned birds I ever had. When she was just a tiny toddler I would bring her in for play. Jake and Judy would try to coax her away and she would follow them to the bird room door. Then I would tap on the floor and call "Come here, Buggles," and she'd hold up both her little wings and paddle back to me as fast as she could. I had talked to her and petted her so much in the box she knew me well, even though I had not hand fed her.

I enjoyed Buggles very much, and she had a nest of three eggs when one of the saddest accidents that ever happened in Birdville befell my cute little pet. She flew from the other room to land at my feet just as I stepped down from a little stool. She was severely injured internally and died in my hands in a few minutes. It is sad when they get sick and die from causes you cannot prevent, but to be the cause of their suffering yourself is far worse. I still use that stool dozens of times every day, but, needless to say, I always go slowly and look before stepping down from it.

CRICKET AND JUNIOR—ACCIDENTS ENDEAR THEM

Cricket was Buggles' little sister but six months younger, and such a pretty little thing with so many yellow flecks on her breast and such a light-gray in color. On her first trial of getting out of the box, she caught a toe fast and broke her leg, flapping and twisting until the leg was nearly twisted off. I set the leg and wrapped and taped it; it was knitting fine, but the swelling hurt her and she chewed all her little toes off, so after that I just had to keep her. She just now came in on my chair, curious as to what this writing is all about. She is a cute, pretty little mother and though it sounds funny, I've raised and shipped a lot of little Crickets all over the country.

Cockies are usually very true to their mates. Photo by Louise Van der Meid.

A yellow-face blue budgerigar. Selective breeding has greatly in-
creased the number of varieties available today. Photo by Mervin
Roberts.

African ringneck parrakeet, blue variety. Photo by Horst Mueller.

Citron-crested cockatoos are distinguished from the other sulphur-crested cockatoos, which they resemble greatly, by a darker, almost orange, color.

Junior, Koxy's first baby, went to live with a neighbor for a while, and my husband brought him home to surprise me as I had been quite ill. I got a bad shock instead of a pleasant surprise. My husband did not know that the cage had a loose tray bottom, and he lifted the cage off and out of his car—and away went Junior out into a dark, stormy night. I heard some excitement downstairs about a bird flying away, and was up off that bed and into coat and slippers and down to see what had happened. I ran back and turned on the bird room lights and opened the windows so if Junior were still in the neighborhood he could hear and see the other birds.

As we thought we heard a call, we listened and watched out there in the rain until we located him on the roof of a house across the street. My son-in-law got a twenty-foot ladder and set it against the house without a thud, and I was up to the roof almost as soon as it hit, but there I stopped and did a bit of sensible thinking. I knew if he saw my head come up over the roof he would be off in a flash, so I began to talk gently, calling him by name and a "pretty boy" and all the "peek-a-boos" and "Bobwhites" and "Whip-poor-wills" I could muster up in my excitement, and then I made the kissing noise I fairly raised them on, and "knocked" on the side of the house as I said it.

I finally heard him answer with a little "cheep;" then and only then did I dare show my head an inch at a time above the roof until I could see him, still not daring to reach for him. I kept talking and knocking on the roof closer and closer until I knew I could grab before he could fly. I made one quick grab and was back down the ladder and back into bed—exhausted. I know I would have been scared to death up that high for any other reason, but I also knew that no one else could catch him, and I had to do all I could. After that I could not bear to sell him and gave him to my daughter. Later, she sold him, and I think of the one who got him never writing so that we would know whether he arrived in good shape and if they liked him or not. . . I always wonder if he got as good a home as he deserved.

A type of cage specially built for a cockatoo. It will also be perfectly suitable for several other types of parrot-like birds like the conure and cockatiel perched on the top of the cage. Photo by Louise Van der Meid.

Half-moon dwarf parrots are noisy, but delightful, birds. They can become great talkers if properly trained at an early age.

ABOUT RAGS—AND A COCKATIEL LOVE TRIANGLE

One baby was such a homely little fellow I just couldn't offer him for sale, so we called him Rags and let him stay here. He soon began to talk and to love me so dearly and, well, he's still here!

A friend had a pair of cockies for years and never could raise any. One day he brought his hen over and said, "Let's trade." He was such a lover of cockies, and I had extras, so his Becky came to Birdville. None of the males would have her, but soon little Rags was old enough and they had nest after nest—but never a fertile egg.

I'd feel sorry about their hard work and no babies, so I'd give them something—perhaps a nest of parrakeets or lovebirds, or a cockie or two, all of which they would raise nicely. One day I thought I would see if wheat-germ oil would help this situation, so I penned them up and really put it to them. Since Buzzie had rested up three or four years after his illness and looked good, I decided to put him in with Rags and Becky to get the benefit of the oils.

In less than three weeks, Buzzie stole Becky's heart, and poor Rags had no lady. Buzzie and Becky went to work in a pretty white bungalow and had three nests. All this time, Rags had to be penned up to keep him from interfering. He was in a pen with grown young ladies and one wanted him to help her raise a nest. They mated and she laid six nice eggs. She would sit so carefully, but Rags would go in and whip her and beat up the nest, finally breaking all the eggs. It seemed to make him so mad that anyone should be sharing his nest besides Becky. The same thing happened with three or four other hens. And every time he would slip out, he would go hunt his Becky. If Buzzie was on the eggs and she happened to be out—she did not mind at all if Rags loved her and scratched her head.

Finally little Woolly grew up and is now Mrs. Woolly Rags and they are very devoted. His new lady and Becky are so alike in looks that most people could not tell them apart. They were both the same size, light gray and "bald-headed." Woolly's parents had picked her so when she was tiny that they must have injured the little bumps where the

Pee-Wee, one of Mrs. Moon's earlier pet cockatiels, occasionally sips left-over coffee.

crest grows, and I doubt that she will ever have one. Becky was bald when she came and still is, although I have used everything I know of to help. Perhaps she was also hurt the same way when she was a baby.

This illustrates how human these birds seem. How they like to choose mates and how badly they hate to lose one— and how fickle some can be. I like Becky, though—she's cute. She won't drink out of regular dishes except when set down fresh. She will go thirsty waiting for us to bring her a fresh drink from the faucet. My husband spoiled her this way —says he can't blame her; he likes fresh clean water too.

Rags, Becky, Karol, Toby, Boy and Buzzie all are gone now. Buzzie died of a heart attack, but had been seemingly well. I was passing some fresh spray millet around that I'd raised myself and the birds loved it so. Buzzie tried to fly to my hand, missed it, and fell to the floor. He was dead when I picked him up. Since he was the one that used to eat at the table with us while Mr. Moon was alive, I missed him terribly. I was living alone in a little cottage in the midst of Parrot Jungle and this was such a loss to me. He sat in a little dish on his corner of the table for two days before I could part with him. That night I lined a little box, removed his pretty wings and tail, and buried him by my doorstep. I sat up most of the night making a beautiful red velvet hat to put the feathers on so I still have my Buzzie. When I left the little cottage, the foil-wrapped boxes of Buzzie and my lovely white cockatoo, Napoleon Bonaparte, were taken up and are now resting by the bird house at Florida's Birdville and are still with me.

Others of my babies and what new owners say

Pretty Boy MacMillan of Dayton, Ohio, says "Pretty Boy," whistles *American Patrol* for his master and has another pretty whistle for the Missus, and a special one for the butler.

Red Sawyer of Norfolk, Virginia, whistles several tunes. He is a grand pet and with his two young babies will make a trio worth showing off to anyone.

Mrs. Trakowski of Richmond taught her Billy a great many words and expressions; he says, "Time to get up, John," when the alarm clock rings.

Cockie LaSage of Huntington has said, ever since he was less than four months old, "Hello, Cockie boy," "How are you?" "I'm all right," "That's fine," and "You're a sweet boy." He calls, "Lucile," when in trouble and says, "No, Cockie," when he is bad. He has a large variety of whistles and can bark like a dog. The hen, Dolly, started at eight months with, "Hello, Cockie," and whistles the same tunes the male does and also the soldier boys' whistle which the male never would do. Now her baby, "Skippy," is saying them all, and he is very young.

Mrs. Mood's bird said, "Hello, Timmie," in three weeks, while his brother didn't say anything for much longer. I believe this is because one bird went to a lady who may have a voice similar to mine, while the other went to a man who was a fine whistler. Naturally the bird was interested in the whistling, but the voice was so different from what he was used to with me that the little fellow was confused.

Evelyn DeBey in Washington, D.C., got Poll-an-Nee. He said quite a few things while here. But although she talked herself hoarse, he never said a word for her for several weeks. Then suddenly one day he talked until he was so excited he could hardly stay on the perch, and he did all the cute things I told her he could do.

Irene Organ's Peter in Memphis is such a fine fellow. I get a Christmas card from them every year. I get a great many Christmas cards from my bird owners and I certainly appreciate them.

Mrs. Gentry in California says her bird sings *Pop Goes the Weasel* and says, "Peek-a-boo, Peachie," "Here, Boogie," to the cat, and likes to play in the cat's fur. I have never seen a cat I would trust that far. A cat killed one lovely baby I had worked hard to train soon after the new owner got it.

Mrs. Eddie Smith of Stroudville, Pennsylvania, thinks so much of her Baby Boy and his mate, What What, that she said if she ever read about them in print she'd get out on the lawn and turn a cartwheel. I hope she doesn't try that, but her birds were so smart that in no time at all Baby Boy was whistling *Rock-A-Bye Baby*, *Red Wing*, and *Over There*. He calls "Baby Boy" and "Hello" all day as plain as she can say it herself. She writes me that she has to do her bird room work with a parrakeet pet on her head, one cockie on her hand and one on her shoulder, each jealous of the others and all wanting a kiss until she gets tired of so much loving. When What What had six eggs she pulled out all Baby Boy's crest and would not let him into the box to set, so the poor fellow tried to drive a pair of 'keets away so he could rear their eight babies.

I didn't hear of all the clever things little Cliffy Kreamer could do and say until after his death, when his owners wrote that no other but a baby from the same parents could ever take his place. As that was impossible (for since Buzzie's serious illness he was not allowed to raise any more) I had to do the next best thing and save them his little half brother.

Then there was little PeeWee, who also met a tragic death. His owner, Alice Dungan, tells me he said "Choo choo car," whenever a train went by. He said "Good morning," when his cage was uncovered in the morning. He whistled *Reveille*, *Pop Goes the Weasel*, and *We're in the Army Now*. At Christmas time he learned *Jingle Bells* in a week. When he was put back in his cage at night he would say crossly, "Good

Talking to your pet assures the bird that you are his or her friend. Start talking to it as early as possible. The tone of your voice should be soft at first, gradually getting stronger as the bird grows up. Photo by George Stewart.

night, nurse," and then make kissing noises as he curled up in his little tomato can bed.

PeeWee was a mischievous fellow. His owner wrote me that there was nothing going on in the kitchen that he wasn't into, taking the seeds out of the apples when she was making an apple pie, and stealing salad out of the salad bowl. When given an empty paper bag on the kitchen table, he amused himself by the hour, pretending it was his private house. She has sent me wonderful snapshots of him sitting on the edge of the cup and having his morning coffee with the family saying, "Good, good" between each sip he would take.

But tragedy came when PeeWee flew on Mrs. Dungan's mother's shoulder just as she was about to step out in the yard— and away he went, screaming, circling, and off over the trees. It was early May and in an hour there was a heavy cold rain. Although they toured the neighborhood in a car and called and called, they never knew what happened to their dear little pet.

A little boy in Montana, Sonny Holm, Jr., earned the money to buy Tommy and loves him dearly. He says, "Hello Tommy" and gets on his daddy's shoulders and pulls out his whiskers and also cuts the snaps and buttons off sister Marjorie's dress.

Bobby, who belongs to Dr. Hecht in Wilmette, Illinois, has solved the doctor's problem of children "not wanting to see the doctor." Now he can't keep them out of his office when Bobby performs his very musical whistles and bird calls. He can imitate the bobwhite, the whippoorwill, and the mourning dove. Miss Braun, the doctor's office assistant, wrote me that recently when the doctor was about to examine a woman patient's heart, Bobby whistled the wolf call "Whew-whoo" in such a knowing way that the patient said, "Your bird is well trained."

Puffer Martin of Cleveland once got away but was good enough to stay in a tree until the hose was brought into play. When soaked, he couldn't fly and was caught again. A few of his words are, "Bad boy," "Be careful there," "Gimme a kiss," and "Call the Kitty, here Kitty, Kitty, Kitty."

Mrs. Marie Gelstrap in Indiana says her Buzzie can say "Peter Piper picked a peck of pickled peppers—a peck of pickled peppers Peter Piper picked," and I think that proves her a top-notch trainer. I can hardly say it myself. She says that her little parrakeet can also say it.

I could go on and on, from hundreds of letters, and tell you the clever things my cockatiels can do and say, but I think this list will satisfy you that a cockatiel *can* talk. I think it proves that they are very smart birds, and if you get a hand tamed bird and do not get worlds of fun out of him— you surely can't have much love for birds, or else you lack all the art of handling and training one.

Others in the Birdville family

As part of my Birdville Family I must say a little about the parrakeet, but I leave most to my good friend Mrs. Kluver, who has written very helpful and complete books on these lively little birds.

I have raised these little fellows as long as I have had cockies, and while I once declared I would never call them such a hard-to-say name as budgerigar, which is their real one, but since I am a member of the American Budgerigar Society I wish to go along with the rest; now that "budgies" seems to be acceptable to all, and I can say that with ease—budgies it will be.

From my first pair I got strange and different colors. I was thrilled with them, but many people at that time were color-breeding budgies, and few appreciated the unusual color combinations. The only extra price I got for them was because I looked at them so often that they became very tame.

A few years later when I wanted some like them I was surprised to find that I would have to pay fifty dollars. They had red eyes when born and kept them when grown—cinnamons are born with red eyes, but they turn dark by the time they come out of the nest. I tried to locate some of my old stock and did locate what I thought was a hen—but it was from another family, so I just had to buy a pair and start all over again.

I now have lutinos and albinos, which are plain yellow and plain white with red eyes (not a mark on backs or wings), and opalines in green and blue. They are marked differently and have more body color on wings and back, and the cap color goes on down the neck. Now for the first time I have what I have worked toward for two years—one blue and one green cinnamon opaline.

I love the fallows too, as they have color and markings and red eyes. It is a job to band and keep records on these, but the thrill of discovering new colors is worth it. I don't band many of the normal colors, since most of them are sold for pets and talkers.

These birds talk wonderfully well—*if* they are picked from especially forward males, weaned earlier than if with parents, and taken away from all others of their own kind as soon as possible. They should be taken between the age of six weeks and three months. If they are talked to, they will positively talk in six weeks to three months after they leave here.

A pair of light green parrakeets. Green is a basic color found in wild birds. Photo by Harry V. Lacey.

Some have been known to recite four verses of a poem or a long string of words and sentences. They like to have a mirror to talk to and talk when they hear the sound of running water. So your pet will do a lot of chattering while you wash dishes or for the Mister when he shaves in the morning. I know of one budgie who was so afraid of not getting to help that he'd watch the bathroom door and make for it the minute the man arose from his chair. My Dicky Bird, whom I left with my daughter in Ohio when I came to Florida, died a year ago. He was twelve years old and a fine talker. He was sold as one of my babies to a lady who was an expert at teaching birds to talk, which I'm not. She got tired of him, imagine, and sold him back to me. We wrote down over 200 words he said; the list is still in my big scrap book. He learned so many new words that I got tired of writing them down. He even came up with: "Hello, cowboy, how are you?" before he died. He must have heard it on T.V., because he loved to watch.

For the small amount spent it would be hard to find anything to equal a hand tamed budgie. I seldom hand feed these little fellows, for I can't charge enough to make the extra work worthwhile, but they can be trained nicely without it. I do it only when there is some special reason, as in the fall when I move some breeders in off the porch and find babies in boxes. Unless taken when so tiny, they are generally about as stubborn to teach to eat from a feeder as a calf to drink out of a bucket—and I have trained many calves also.

I do so enjoy having my birds loved and appreciated that I am going to include a letter I just received:

"Dear Mrs. Moon:

"According to your records I will be one year old next Sunday. I am healthy and sound—never an illness since birth. I am always cheerful and never still a moment. I have lots of toys, marbles, swings, bells, etc., and play all day—so happy in my home and try to make others happy too. I'll send you my picture as soon as Mr. Rolle takes one.

"I can say, 'Good morning, Topper,' 'give me a big kiss, make it smack,' 'I love you sweetheart, Albert,' and lots of other words. I did not know what you might like for a re-

Mrs. Moon coaxing Mr. Hopper (a greater sulphur-crested cockatoo) to hold his wings open for this photo.

membrance on my birthday, so I am asking Mr. Rolle to send you a check to buy something you especially like, for they say the happiness and comfort I have brought can't be measured in wordly goods. Then whenever you see it you can think of little Topper Rolle in Wilmette, Illinois."

Yes, Topper, that is just what I'll do—a gift to me is not just something to have and own, it is a reminder of the one who gave it, and each time I see it I enjoy again our association. And, Topper, did you know that September eleventh is my birthday, too. So when you are a year old I will be fifty-seven years old.

A number of the following beautiful and more rare birds are also classified as parrakeets, even my beloved cockatiels—another reason that it is best to use the name budgie for the little shell parrakeet. But don't make the mistake of calling them lovebirds. The lovebird is an entirely different and larger bird. I correct this confusing mistake whenever possible.

RED RUMP. . .

This is also a very lovely bird—smaller and shorter than a cockie and easily sexed, since the male is much more colorful. This bird is a very desirable addition to any aviary or home if it is tamed.

ELEGANT. . .

This is one of the prettiest of the group—small—not much larger than a big budgie. They are pretty shades of green, some with yellow shadings and a bit of blue arranged on the face that makes them look like they are wearing spectacles.

HOODED PARRAKEET. . .

These are "just out of this world" and very rarely raised in captivity.

The body is a beautiful turquoise blue with about one-half of the wing canary yellow. The back is black, and they wear a black cap. To be displayed at their best they should have plenty of flight space, in which they resemble gorgeous butterflies flying about. They are a little larger than the elegants.

BARNARDS. . .

These are equally as beautiful, with a bluish green body with a tinge of yellow. The wing shoulders are a brilliant blue. Larger and heavier than a cockie.

MEALY ROSELLA. . .

For one who prefers soft blending and pastel colors, these birds are truly lovely, blues and grays with prettily shaded spots on their backs. The heads are almost pure yellow. Some say they look like a bald eagle, but I don't like that description; they do not look ferocious but mild and kind and are much more so than many other birds. My two were three or four months old when I got them. They had been raised in a large flight and not handled. They seemed dissatisfied in any place I put them, so I decided not to wait

107

Three members of the Birdville "family"—a small Amazon parrot, Romeo, a red macaw, and a red female electus parrot.

until they raised their young in order to get some that I could hold—I would hold these.

I cut their wings and brought them into the living room every evening for their exercise. Now they will step up on my hand, ride on my shoulder, or sit on a perch-stand by the mirror. They have several very beautiful calls and are not noisy. They like to roam around and did once climb up the curtain and completely ruin a blind, so now I watch them a little closer. In disposition I consider them a close second to cockies. They get along nicely together.

STANLEY ROSELLA. . .

The male has a ruby-red body with a yellow bib, olive back, blue wings, and is nearly the size of a cockie, although both the rosellas have a larger head, slightly heavier body, and no crest. The Stanley is a little smaller than the mealy.

RED CAPS OR PILEATED. . .

The body is a dark lilac, with a green back and wings and a beautiful red cap. They are a little larger than the mealy rosellas and can raise their head feathers like a crest.

RINGNECKS. . .

A pair of large African ringneck parrakeets are very beautiful. They are the size of a small parrot, but more slenderly shaped, and they have very long tails. The male has a dark ring edged with salmon pink around his neck.

They are very noisy, but if I could hand tame a nest of them they would be lovely. My pair laid, but I disposed of them before ever getting babies.

CONURES OR DWARF PARROTS. . .

There are many kinds of these—all can make quite a lot of noise. I wondered if I dared keep mine after I got them. In fact, I did not tell anyone I was getting them until they were here, as I did not want them condemned unseen. They *are* noisy, but my husband is so kind—he doesn't care so much for the birds, but he surely does for me, so he puts up with them. So far, he says they have not bothered him, and we do not think they annoy the neighbors.

I have one pair of black-hooded pink stockings—or Nandays. They are dark green with black heads and have a bit of rosy red where the feathers join the legs. I also have one pair of Jendays. They are green with quite a little red and orange on head and face—and a little scattered low on the breast and some on the wings and tail.

A pair of little half-moons are finger tame, smart as can be, and don't bite, but they look at me as if they would like to see if they could bluff and boss me. I got them to understand—No, not here! They can make enough noise for ten birds but are just as cute as they can be. I kept only one and she talks quite well, and says, "Hi Connie, what you want, huh?" "You're a pretty boy, yes, you are," "Give me a kiss, a great big kiss," and "Peek-a-boo." When she is out on my shoulder she pesters me for kisses by grabbing my lips and pulling me around, or she pinches my ear. When she pinches too hard she immediately says, "No, no, bad boy, bad boy." She can say "girl" but usually says "boy."

She loves me a lot and seems to like some strangers, but others seem to stir up all the meanness in her and she is ready for a fight. To get my cockies to whistle the wolf call, I say "pere-eet whee-er" and they whistle it as well as any soldier could, but Connie says it just as I do.

COCKATOOS. . .

Polly is a greater white sulphur-crested, one of the most wonderful of birds and simply beautiful. Her white feathers shine like satin and she is so gentle—she can be taken up in one's arms and hugged like a baby. She can follow any tune on the piano by whistling it, and she dances and talks.

Another white one, a lesser sulphur-crested, was a female. She was somewhat spoiled. She laid five to seven eggs every May, set on them, and loved them so much. I traded her for eight baby wild cockatiels. When I took her to the depot to be shipped to California she said, "Poor Polly, poor, poor Polly," in the most pitiful voice. She went all the way to California and then was sold to the Art Institute in Dayton, Ohio, coming back across the continent again.

Tommy was a big rose-breasted cockatoo—no one knew how old he was. He had been knocked around from home to home or pet shop, living in all kinds of unsuitable cages and on bad food until he looked somewhat motheaten. As usual, he finally got around to me after he was so ugly and so run down no one else would have him. I made him a stand out of wire to sit on, which he could climb on easily and had room to flap his wings and preen his feathers. I fed him well and gave him cod-liver oil. He soon shed out and was very pretty. But as he gained more strength and pep he became a little too sassy to my cockies, so I found him a fine home in an outdoor aviary where I think he finished out his life in peace.

For just a little while I had two sweet baby ones like him. They were adorable, and I hated to give them up. They will no doubt breed when two years old as they never knew what it was to fly in an aviary. They will need a huge grandfather clock-style box of heavy material, for they can really chew things up when they want a nest. They have several shades of soft gray on their back with the richest deep rose breast. They can raise these head feathers although when not raised they do not show at all. This is what is meant by "pileated."

A pair of lorikeets. Photo by Louise Van der Meid.

A pair of orange-crested cockatoos were the pride of my life. They were about half-way between the greater and lesser sulphur-crested in size, and their crests were a deep orange, and very beautiful. I longed to raise a nest of them so I could hold them, as mine were wild, but I did not have enough room for such large birds. Their noise worried my poor sick husband, and since he was bravely putting up with a lot of noise with all the others, I felt that I should let them go. But I enjoyed them for a while, and really, to see them courting and in display over their nest box was a wonderful sight to me.

LORIES. . .

These beauties are my prize possessions. Besides their gorgeous colorings, they are playful. They run, jump, and hop stiff-legged up and down, bowing and bobbing their heads, or wrestle on the floor like two little boys. Sometimes one lies flat on his back while the other runs around him chewing his feet.

The head is a purplish blue with a light green ring around the back of the neck; the back, wings, and tail are green. In front, below the blue throat, the breast is of brilliant red mixed with a few orange feathers, followed by a band of purplish blue; a few of the red and orange feathers are sprinkled on the sides, around the legs and tail. The colors seem to tie into each other by having borders of the red on some of the first blue ones, or blue borders on some of the red. The bill is bright red. The tongue is different from that of any other hook-bill; it is longer and not quite so wide. It seems brush-like when they want it to be. This is to lap up the milk and honey they live on, together with fruit and soaked bread (they eat no seed). They have a nice disposition and come to drink their honey out of the cup while I hold it. They can lap it up as fast as a kitten or puppy.

One of them is trained to roll over on his back to show his pretty tummy Whenever he hears strangers come in, he gets restless and anxious to get his job over with. Pacing around, he watches me until I get the little stool down by the door, then he comes down by the side of the cage and over to the corner, rolls over on his back, and holds my fingers with his feet until I take him out and show him off. Then he runs back, as if to say, "Well, that's over with."

REDBIRDS. . .

One year a storm blew a nest of tiny redbirds out into the water-filled yard of a neighbor. Two were drowned before they were found. The other two were brought to me. I hand fed them, and they grew like little weeds. Both of them were females. They were very mischievous and carried off everything they could drag. When one day my little glass feeder was carried in from the kitchen and dropped at my

Cockatoos, such as this sulphur crested cockatoo sitting beside a cockatiel, can be trained to dance, talk, and perform tricks for an audience. Photo by Louise Van der Meid.

feet, they had to be banned to the bird porch.

Before they were full-grown they began to quarrel with each other, first one bossing the situation and then the other, so that they could not live in the same room, so I had to let one go. The other one made no attempt to nest the next year (she was an August-hatched bird), but the second year by April first she had a lovely nest all made and laid four eggs in an old Christmas tree I fastened up in the corner of the porch.

Quail, too, have a place in Birdville. This bird was photographed by the breeder, Ian Herman.

She lets me stroke her back and feed her meal worms while on the nest. Chipper finally went to live in a zoo after I gave up the special permit I had for wild birds. Now I take only orphaned wild babies and hand feed them to save their lives. When they are old enough to eat alone, a zoo is more than glad to receive the gift, and I think it much better than turning them loose, for many would die after all my work to save them. Then they are also more satisfied than wild-captured ones, and people can enjoy them more.

Since it was so hard for me to give up redbirds, I was more than glad to find some imported from South America that I can keep. They are about as pretty in color, but not in face and expression, somehow. I have yet to see our American cardinal's equal. The bill is larger and black (horn color) instead of red. The male has fewer black feathers, the crests are quite different, and the song not as good. To some they don't fill the bill at all, but since in many states not even those imported from Mexico are allowed to be caged, I think it is nice to find some that we can have and enjoy.

QUAIL. . .

Old Valley and his mate are two lovely quail from California with beautiful curved plumes on their heads. He has a high-stepping, proud walk and stands watch while she sets. When disturbed he calls Kuk-kuk-ku-wak, Kuk-kuk-ku-wak!

Quailie is a dear little bobwhite hatched out by old Koxy cockatiel and raised under an aquarium lamp. His brother drowned in his drinking water, although it was only a pop bottle cap, so I put quarter inch mesh over it and got this one through. He lies on his back in my hand and plays dead. He loves to fight my feet or hands like a bantam rooster, and will generally show off to visitors by saying, "Talk, talk, whip, whip whip-poor-will, whip-poor-will." Most people are completely astonished, but while I have never heard of wild quail talking, they evidently have this ability. I am a poor one to teach birds to talk, but Quailie talks so plainly anyone can understand it.

Very recently came a pair of California Gambles, also plumed and looking very much like the Valleys. Chixy and Chuck are a pair of tiny Philippine button quails. They don't look as big as a robin on your lawn, for they have very short tails. The neck and legs are also short. They are as quick as lightning and marked so prettily. They like it better out on the porch in the leaves and brush and make little nests and lay a clutch of eight to twelve large greenish brown eggs, large as a cockie's, but the little male usually eats them before time to hatch.

When he finds an egg or a meal worm or anything good, he calls and calls the hens. He won't eat it until they come. If they are kept in a cage they get frightened at night and fly up and bruise their heads. If a shipping box is not padded they often arrive completely scalped, so if kept in a cage their wings should be cut.

JAVA SPARROW OR RICE BIRD. . .

I get many a smile from the personalities and antics of my birds. Recently I found a pair of rice birds sitting together between a pair of blue Mexican ground doves. The male rice bird would stroke and love his mate for a while, and then turn and love and fix the feathers of the little dove on the other side of him. Life is never dull in Birdville.

The Java rice sparrow, often called "rice bird," is a very pretty and quite hardy little bird, a bit larger than a canary. The natural colors of these birds are steel gray coats, snow white cheeks, rosy gray chest and stomach, black satin heads, and black tail. These colors, together with a large cherry-red beak, make a very striking little bird. They are also bred in pure white or calico but retain their bright red beaks. The calicos are a mixture of the natural gray and the white.

They are very easy to hand-feed and make cute affectionate pets. I once raised three ricers with eight cockies, and when the cockies were nearly full size the rice birds were afraid of getting stepped on, and with good reason, for when eight cockies are hungry and see their feeder coming, they really stamp around. So the little ricers would hop on the cockies' backs where they could more easily reach the feeder and would lean way over and clean up the feed on the cockies' faces. They liked to crawl in among the cockies to keep warm at night, even after they were flying about. This was all right if it happened to be some of their eight friends, but very few of the other cockies would tolerate it, and there would be a battle, for the rice bird is quite sassy.

Sometimes, if I am sitting still, writing, they come and cuddle up in my left hand to take their nap. I sold a little male to a young girl in Illinois who wrote me that "Mooie" would not settle down for the night unless he first fell asleep in the palm of her hand. I wonder how many realize what an unusual thrill it is to be able to hold that warm bit of fluff in your hand and know how utterly it trusts you. They have a wild, sweet song and use it generously—it reminds you of woodlands and running streams and the whole mystery of nature.

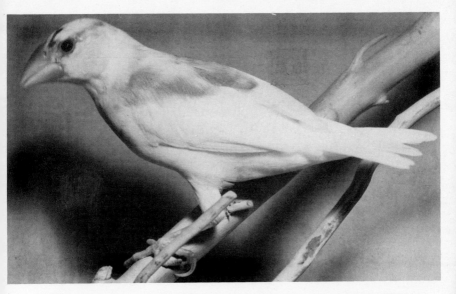

Shown is a calico Java rice bird, one of the varieties of the Java rice bird developed in captivity. The color markings are extremely variable and no two birds are exactly alike.

ZEBRA FINCHES

I have a number of white, gray, and silver zebra finches loose in the bird room with coconut shells, boxes, and little places fixed all around for them to nest in. These birds seldom hand feed; like the budgerigars, they are not worth the effort involved. But I certainly do enjoy their cute antics and to have them fly on my head and pull at my hair to try to get material for their large sparrow-like nests.

I recently made the mistake of wearing a hair net in the bird room. Five minutes later it was gone. The next time I came to the bird room, I noticed two male zebras flapping about on the floor. I first thought a lovebird had broken their legs or wings and went to pick one up, and the other came along. They were wound up in the hair net, so I had to cut it all to pieces to free them. They had stolen it to make their nest. They fill up their boxes to overflowing with anything they can drag into it, and a dozen of these little birds often fly to the dish of bread and milk to eat. They make a pretty picture. The babies lie flat down on the floor and just turn up their pretty heads to be fed, instead of standing up high to reach for the food.

OTHER FINCHES. . .

My parson finch, with his black clerical vest and spectacles, is a spry little fellow with a very weird call. When I turn on a light to shine out into the bird porch or very early in the morning when dawn is coming up, his call is enough to set the cockies on a stampede. Like the Javas, the smooth beauty of his feathers more than compensates for anything he otherwise lacks. Shaft-tails look almost like the Parson, except they have much longer and very pointed tails.

I have given up trying to breed the little strawberry finches. They don't want to lay eggs until nearly fall, and by then it gets cool at night and the hen gets egg-bound so easily. They are cute and sing a sweet little song; the hen sings nearly as well as the male. The painted finches are like larger versions of the strawberry but do not have as sweet a song. Both are prettier than the more rare green strawberry.

Gouldians are the most beautiful of all finches. They look like a bouquet of flowers or a pretty patchwork quilt. The colors are not blended together, but one joins the other in sharp outlines. This bird has a red head (some are black), a purple and gold breast and a green back. However, their song is negligible, hardly more than that of the little society finches, who make up for lack of volume in many queer dances and cute actions. Gouldians and cutthroats also dance to their ladies.

A paradise whydah (about the size of a canary) was just a plain tan and gray fellow a month ago. Today he is white and black and tinged with burnt orange and has a gracefully curved tail over a foot long. Weavers are also in plain clothes part of the year, but in breeding season they come into beautiful coats and weave nests in the branches, which they seldom use.

The rainbow finches are colorful little birds. They have a short sweet song not unlike a few cardinal notes. However, they seldom sing except just at daybreak, or if a bright light shines on them suddenly during the night. The breast is orange and golden yellow, the back a bright blue, and the head is green.

MY ZOO FAMILY. . .

Hearing of a little zoo that was discontinuing its bird collection, I put in my bid, got and brought home to an already crowded apartment seven macaws, four cockatoos and several others. I was just too happy to sleep and walked from one to the other, just looking and loving for another hour. Then I happened to think—my birthday. I still say that's the most wonderful birthday gift I ever had, even if I did buy it myself! And during these lonely years, with my dear companion gone, they have been my life. They are: Big Mack—a hyacinthine lady who loves me so much she doesn't want me to go to sleep. It would be all right if she could sleep on a bed with me; she doesn't talk. Milly, a lady; Mom, a boy; Pop, a lady; Rita, a boy—four scarlet macaws, all talk; two greater sulphur-crested cockatoos, a true pair, Lady and Miss Kramer—who was cover boy on a national magazine and likes to go on TV. He shows off to all visitors by hopping with crest up, ringing a bell and (for pay) asking for a drink, which he takes from the edge of a glass. He lets anyone hold and pet him, has nice table manners and sits in one corner, waiting until given his dish. He wants to be fed orange juice with a spoon. He talks softly and sweetly. These birds were great attractions at the national shows and brought me beautiful trophies, ribbons and rosettes.

If you lose a fine pet, never say that you'll never get another one. I lost my Miss Kramer very suddenly, and I never knew the cause. Lady came south with me and laid thirty eggs, but Big Boy ate all but one of them. The one remaining egg hatched, and I hand fed the baby until it feathered. It was the dearest creature I ever beheld, but it died with a hemorrhage without warning. My next darling was Napoleon Bonaparte, who met a heartbreaking death. Now Mr. Hopper is my pride and joy; he puts on a show for all the visitors—a million dollars couldn't buy him from me. As long as he and I live, he'll be with me. Think of the joy and happiness I'd have missed if I'd said, "Never another."

Shipping off to new owners

When a little bird, for whom someone has been waiting a long time, perhaps even before he was hatched, is finally ready for shipping, there is still work to be done. If it is not done, all the previous work of feeding and taming will have been in vain.

The bird is caged alone for a while to check droppings to see whether he is in perfect condition for his journey. He is usually encouraged to drink from the shipping water fountain so he will recognize it and know how to drink from it. The express company is called to get a routing so that he need not wait in a station for hours before train time, but will be shipped out and arrive at his destination in the shortest possible time. He is provided with plenty of food for the trip, even allowing for delays. If any special feed or care is needed on arrival, a note is enclosed or tacked on his box in plain sight, although I have had boxes come back to me from the new owners with my note still on. Some people are not very curious. I ship by air if port to port, but rail and air charges where there is no port are very expensive, so I usually ship straight express unless the customer agrees to the added expense.

Birds must be insured to full value, otherwise the express company will not pay over a certain dollar value for each bird, even if through their mishandling the bird is lost, stolen or accidentally killed. Overvaluing increases the customer's charges, but he should be willing to pay for full insurance, as the shipper must be protected and he wants his bird to arrive in good shape.

For the same reason, the box should be as light as possible, yet strong and safe. Also it must be wrapped to suit the weather. If it is cold weather, I wrap it in paper with a cellophane window for light and only small holes for air, being careful that the holes are protected in such a way that another box can't be set flat on or against the holes and the air cut off. Some shipping boxes have slanted wire openings so it is impossible to set anything on top or push anything against it and cut the air off. If the wire is across the front, I have a hole or two on the top and the rope handle prevents the holes from being closed up.

Expressmen prefer a handle or the box tied with strong twine so they can grasp it easily and quickly with one hand, for they often have to change the contents of a whole car in very short time. I watch all corners and nails so that nothing catches or tears the hands or clothing of those handling the box.

Female redrump parrakeet.

For a long trip I use a removable drinker, for if it gets filled with food, unless the messenger can remove it from the box, he is helpless to do anything but add more water. Then the bird may arrive sick and poisoned from the foul slimy water. I have received birds from a long distance with water so foul it made me sick to smell it. In fact, I can tell by how thirsty they are on arrival they have gone without water rather than drink it. So I do not risk this with my precious cockies.

Neither do I trust my birds to express delivery trucks from my home. I take the box myself to the train just a half hour ahead of time. I write up all papers myself so they are legible and just the way the express company wants it done. I put on the cage, "Feed Enclosed for Entire Trip If Kept This Side Up. Please Check Water Daily." There is a livestock card attached and there is a place on it for shipper's instructions, so I use it. I see that "Water Daily" is on the shipping instructions, and if it is a removable can, I tell them how to remove it.

If the bird is being shipped C.O.D. there is a special place for shipper's instructions regarding it. I always put on "If For Any Reason Not Accepted, Do Not Write or Phone— Return at Once." The reason for this precaution is that one lady just didn't have the money when the bird arrived, so there were express charges both ways and a long distance telephone call to pay, and the poor little bird subjected to two tiring trips. Fortunately for my birds, this has never happened to me, but it has happened to other breeders. I have profited by their experiences by refusing to accept C.O.D.'s on birds unless I have received sufficient deposit money to cover such risk. Don't blame any shipper who does not welcome C.O.D.'s without sufficient deposit. I have heard that C.O.D.'s are handled more carefully, but the express company positively denies this, and I have not found it to be true.

I always put two address tags on a crate and try to have my name and address on the crate itself. I have been in the station when a shipment has arrived with all labels soaked off or lost, and what a problem the transport people have to know what to do with the shipment. I would not want that to happen to one of my babies.

Most of my customers appreciate the effort I make to satisfy them and are careful to clean and dry my water fountain and crate and return them promptly; they write at once to ease my mind on the safe arrival and that they are pleased with the bird. I more than appreciate this courtesy. But I am sorry to say there are a few who break up the crate in opening it, send it back with the water still in the can to rust it and the feed left in it to be strewn all over the expressman's truck or car, or paste labels all over my painted signs.

But worse still are the ones who do not return the crate at all, although asked repeatedly to just call their local expressman and return it at my expense. However, I am glad to say there are not many people who like birds enough to want one for themselves who are as negligent as this.

Don't forget to check droppings—the diary of your bird's health. Also take note of any marked difference in the amount of food eaten.

Don't fill a hand fed baby bird too full and upset his digestion. You be the judge, not the baby. He will keep on crying for more even when full.

Don't forget his grit and vitamins, and remember that you can make him sick on these if dosed too heavily. Measure carefully.

Don't forget that carrots supply more vitamin A than any other food. Birds will not overeat after weaning, so offer plenty.

Don't cook too much gruel at a time or mix too much oil food.

Don't use the regular cod-liver oil unless you use it in a way to distribute it well or the birds may get too much oil. It is best to use the concentrated cod-liver oil of which a few drops are equal to a half teaspoonful of regular oil. One drop a day is plenty for each bird.

Don't neglect the hen's bath whenever she wants it, especially toward the last incubation period. The little fellows in the eggs may be too dry to get out and all her work is lost.

Don't worry if the hen does not lay as soon as you think she ought to. You can't hurry her. Some are very deliberate. Just keep offering everything to make eggs and shells and make her comfortable and happy—then add patience.

Don't throw eggs away too soon—eighteen days, but some don't start setting at once. If alive the chick will "kick" when put in a cup of warm water, but only leave the egg there for a few minutes or he will drown. With the proper moisture the baby turns round and round, pushing at the shell as he goes. When thus "pipped" all around he literally "pops" out, leaving the shell in two neat pieces as if cut.

Don't let two members of the family try to teach your bird to say the same words. Different voices confuse birds, and they are really only mimicking you. Either have one person do all the teaching or have each one teach a different thing. Then repeat and repeat.

Don't worry if your bird opens his mouth and stretches

and crooks his neck. He is not choking or swallowing something, just yawning and exercising his throat muscles. Others have a queer little habit of shaking their heads constantly when you talk to them.

Don't believe that your bird will never have mites. They will get on anything with feathers. But they are thick, indeed, if they stay on the bird during the day. So check the cage, box, or nest and do not let the birds be tortured. Watch the ends of perches and cover the cage at night with white cloth on which the tiny red mites can be seen easily as they crawl off the bird.

Don't put the cage in a draft. More birds are killed this way than any other. And putting them in the hot sun is equally as bad.

Don't forget that grit is your bird's "teeth"—supply plenty.

Don't forget that water in a shallow dish warms quickly.

Don't think your bird will not fly away. This warning cannot be repeated too often. Little Dolly rode all the way to California on the shoulder of her mistress, who was offered one hundred and fifty dollars for her tame bird. She often came here for seeds and I'd fairly shudder and beg her not to risk it. Then one evening not three feet from the back door that she had gone in and out of hundreds of times—Dolly took off—being frightened by a dog. Her mistress cried and hunted and called all night, but there was never a trace of Dolly.

Don't forget to be watchful as you go through doors on the inside also. One fine talker was killed by the owner that way; he was trying to follow her and the door closed on him.

I receive letters and S.O.S. calls from everywhere. I am addressed as Dear Sir often, and Mr. and Mrs. Birdville, and recently as "Dear Mrs. Cockatiel." My post office brought an envelope marked "Mrs. Cockatiel—raises birds, Springfield, Ohio." No street, no zone, no name. So I think our Uncle Sam is pretty nice to us bird lovers. So now, won't *you* please be nice to me and guard the baby we've both loved so.

INDEX

Page numbers printed in **bold** refer to photographs and illustrations.